CIRCLE OF LOVE OVER DEATH

TESTIMONIES OF THE MOTHERS OF THE PLAZA DE MAYO

MATILDE MELLIBOVSKY

Translated by
Maria & Matthew Proser

CURBSTONE PRESS

FIRST EDITION, 1997
Copyright © 1997 by Matilde Mellibovsky
Translation Copyright © 1997 by Maria & Matthew Proser
All Rights Reserved

Special thanks to Neil Curri and Barbara Rosen for their help
with this book.

Printed in the U.S. on acid-free paper by BookCrafters
Cover design & illustration: Stephanie Church

Curbstone Press is a 501(c)(3) nonprofit publishing house
whose programs are supported in part by private donations
and by grants from: ADCO Foundation, Witter Bynner
Foundation for Poetry, Connecticut Commission on the Arts,
Connecticut Arts Endowment Fund, The Ford Foundation,
The Greater Hartford Arts Council, Junior League of
Hartford, Lawson Valentine Foundation, LEF Foundation,
Lila Wallace-Reader's Digest Literary Publishers Marketing
Development Program administered by CLMP, The Andrew
W. Mellon Foundation, National Endowment for the Arts,
Puffin Foundation, and United Way-Windham Region.

Library of Congress Cataloging-in-Publication Data

Mellibovsky, Matilde.
     [Circulo de amor sobre la muerte. English]
     Circle of love over death : mothers of the Plaza de Mayo / by
Matilde Mellibovsky : translated by Maria and Matthew Proser.
        p.   cm.
     ISBN 1-880684-38-1
     1. Madres de Plaza de Mayo (Association)   2. Disappeared
persons—Argentina. I. Title.
HV6322.3.A7M4513
323.4'9'0982—dc20   96-24501

published by
CURBSTONE PRESS   321 Jackson Street   Willimantic, CT 06226
     phone: (860) 423-5110   e-mail: curbston@connix.com
           http://www.connix.com/~curbston/

CONTENTS

FOREWORD by Antonio Elio Brailovsky / *i*

THE NEED FOR A BOOK / *viii*

ARRIVING AT THE PLAZA / *xiii*

CHAPTER 1: THE CHILDREN
Let Those Who Want to Hear, Listen / 1
Testimonies:
    Poema Gardella de Akerman / 8
    Lola Weinschelbaum de Rubino / 11
    María Adela Gard de Antokoletz / 15
    Lidia Miy Uranga de Almeida / 20

CHAPTER 2: THE MOTHERS CONFRONT
               THE DISAPPEARANCES
I Want to Mine the Earth until I Find You / 25
Testimonies:
    Elida Busi de Galletti / 32
    Esther Aracela Lado de Sanchez / 43

CHAPTER 3: THE SEARCH AND THE WAIT
Let Them Give Us Hope... / 52
Testimonies:
    Carmen Robles de Zurita / 64
    Fanny Brener de Bendersky / 70
    Enriqueta Maroni / 77

CHAPTER 4: THE MOTHERS GO TO THE PLAZA
A Circle of Love / 82
Testimonies:
    Marta Vázquez / 90
    Angelica P. Sosa de Mignone / 103
    Josefina Gandolfi de Salgado / 106

CHAPTER 5: THE STRUGGLE AND THE
        DICTATORSHIP
What Else Is There to Do, What Else Is There to
    Try? We Were Born Again.... / 116
Testimonies:
    Carmen Aguiar de Lapaco / 138
    Camern Isabel Rodino de Cobo / 152
    Gladys Castro de Lepiscopo / 156

CHAPTER 6: DEMOCRACY ARRIVED
One Waited Full of Hope / 160
Testimonies:
    Ilda Irrustita de Miccucci / 182
    Sara Silver de Brodsky / 187
    Alicia Rivarola de Cárdenas / 193

CHAPTER 7: THE MOTHERS TODAY
    Why Do We Continue the Circle? / 200
Testimony of Maria Isabel Choborik de Mariani / 205

Testimonies:
    Elena Dubrovsky de Pasik / 216
    Matilde Saidler de Mellibovsky / 221

EPILOGUE / 243

Notes: NAMES & TERMS / 247

CIRCLE OF LOVE OVER DEATH

FOREWORD

Who among us has not talked to her children about that longest of rainy afternoons when she burnt books, magazines and letters, and changed her address book so that certain names would not appear? Or about that time when she was stopped on the street and they put a gun to her chest, but luckily she had her identity papers.

Time gnaws at the memory of us grown-ups. Perhaps we believe the horror we have lived through will not be repeated. Or perhaps we think it has all been a nightmare, an error, a bad dream better quickly forgotten. Who among us dares tell our children about that feeling of oppression we felt in our chests when we heard the sirens at night, and the enormous silence that surrounded them, our breath held until the sound died away in the darkness? No, they didn't stop here! They keep on going today; and we sigh a breath of relief when we hear the shots far in the distance.

Do your children and mine know the names of the friends we lost in those dark years? I have to confess to you I did not talk to my children about Graciela Mellibovsky's fathomless eyes, about Rafael Perrotta's journalistic endeavors or about Amalia Moavro's passion for the opera.

No, our children don't know anything about all this. Are we protecting them, or is it that we don't dare show them our own fear? What has overtaken us that we forget so easily? Perhaps some blind faith that history cannot repeat itself?

On December 1st, 1828, General Lavalle rebelled against the constitutional government and executed Governor Manuel Dorrego.

"It was necessary" was his sole explanation. "He would have brought chaos."

Today what the name Juan Lavalle means to us is a street full of movie houses, a space where frivolousness makes us forget the crime. There each evening people submerge themselves in countless fictitious crimes, forgetting the original real one, that of a dictator and the shots that gave his name to a street.

Memories, things forgotten. Lavalle is a coffee house, a slice of pizza, a popular movie actor, a naked woman on a screen.

Jorge Luis Borges speaks of a famous murderer in Palermo whose wife still kept his weapon on her night table because for her the knife stood for the man: "Juan Murana who walked on streets familiar to me, who knew what men know, who was conversant with the taste of death and who later became a knife and then the memory of a knife and tomorrow would become oblivion, plain ordinary oblivion." I ask myself about the way in which our children will remember another knife, Luciano Benjamin Menendez's dagger.

I have just finished teaching my class in a high school. I was talking about crimes in general and in passing I mentioned the name of a prototypical criminal. The students continued to look at me, disconcerted: "Who is Jorge Rafael Videla?" they asked me, and for a moment I did not know how to respond, but Matilde does know and that is why she wrote this book—so that the collective memory does not forget.

Matilde speaks of an era that we all would prefer to forget, but she convinces us of the value of memory. Freud shows us how the person who does not understand his past is condemned to repeat it. Thus, I remember my own youthful astonishment when I learned about the executions in Patagonia. At that time I concluded that Patagonia was very far away and that 1921 was even further away.

It was in the 1960's. I was 20 years old and all terrors seemed to me very distant. I used to read about Nazism and could not imagine how it was possible that an entire country—the learned German people—could have silently accepted the creation of a regime of terror. I used to look at the daily newspapers, the black and white pictures, with a vague feeling of unreality: in Germany, in Italy, in Poland, in France, men, women and even babies at the breast disappeared without anyone noticing, while the suspicion of the extermination camps grew like a shadow.

On the contrary, we were secure. This was a democratic country and nothing like that could be imagined here.

That is why Matilde shows us that the right to life and to speech, to ideas and to justice, is not merely a gift we must graciously receive, but an objective to fight for every day of our lives. Are we prepared to listen to this voice that speaks to us about the immense fragility of the pluralistic democracy in which we believe today?

Why another book for a society in which every form of horror has already been described? Because perhaps we have not talked enough, when we now take into account those who opportunistically supported reconciliation.

But besides, this is a unique book because of what it tells us and because of the way in which it was written. One of its main characters manages to gain some distance from the story, and then she begins to narrate it.

To tell it, the author uses a narrative method which parallels the actual happenings it represents. To this collective voice individual voices are joined. The mothers tell their experiences while the book is itself being shaped. There are no prepared questions, there are no preconceived outlines. Each encounter is a conversation, not a news report.

The author is not a newspaper woman, and she has not made any effort to appear to be one. She uses the language of daily life, everyday words, not a professional vocabulary. The result is a work with a collective main character, written in the manner of Andre Malraux or of the films of Eisenstein. The facts spring up from a chorus of voices, not a soloist. In this book there are no bosses or leaders, just a group of women who confront a dictatorship with bare hands.

Matilde gathers these voices one by one with infinite respect for their diversity and for the individual nuances with which each one meets the common suffering. And as we advance in the reading, there is an aspect that surprises us: all the mothers interviewed are experienced painters of political reality; that is to say, they are able to evaluate interconnections and to make decisions. Under differing circumstances, each of them can represent the group and speak for all of it.

Furthermore, to talk about the Mothers of the Plaza de Mayo is also to talk about the dictatorship that created them, and its characteristics, about which we Argentinians cannot come to agreement. That is why I want to stress that the last dictatorship's objective was to change the form of the country, to carry us to the Argentina which we inhabit today: economically smaller, politically more conformist, and socially more unjust.

To achieve this, it was necessary to kill many people who thought differently and who might present an obstacle to their program. Paradoxically, those who talked about defending us from terrorism could not—or would not—gather the evidence to demonstrate that the kidnapped had actually committed the crimes attributed to them. The public trials of the main figures of the dictatorship show that it is possible to gather such proof when it exists and, moreover, when there is the desire to gather it.

Still, no political order is based on crime alone. Every government needs some level of public consensus in order to maintain itself, even a dictatorship. These crimes were committed with the backing of most of the traditional political institutions, who put forward mayors, ambassadors, ministers and secretaries, financiers, bishops, and union representatives; they all were capable of putting more complacent individuals in the jobs of the disappeared, while they achieved international support by exchanging commercial advantages.

One perceives that all the sectors which benefited from the dictatorship worked on public opinion so as to minimize the truth of this political alliance. They did it by means of two concurrent strategies: on the one hand they tried to reduce the image of the dictatorship to its horror alone. That is to say, they tried to make the public forget the political and economic objectives which lay the groundwork for the crimes being committed. This allowed these crimes to be presented as a nightmare and not as the concerted action of the most powerful groups in Argentina.

However, the reduction of the dictatorship to its demons of horror allowed some of these criminals to forgive each other, and people of good conscience to say: "Let us forget this horror and let us reconcile the separated brothers."

It is also worthwhile remembering what daily life was like during the dictatorship. In contrast to the distinctive characteristic of the countries occupied by the Nazis—sadness—many of us lived out the occupation as a time of self-indulgence, the Argentinian "belle epoque." Juan Lavalle is the street of movie houses. Jorge Videla brought us color TVs, encouraged us to win a world soccer championship, offered us travel to foreign lands, and displayed before our eyes the immense marvels of Taiwanese electronics or French cheese. Certainly it was a grand era. We had access to consumer goods of which we had never even dreamt. Next year we might find ourselves in Paris or in Venice, toasting the return of the Malvinas.

Every so often a vague shadow fell across this happiness: there were some people who were no longer among us to enjoy the imported cars or gadgets of whose very use we were ignorant.

Someone or other contrived a vague answer: "There must have been some reason," he'd say making a vague gesture with his hand, and many of us repeated that certainly there must have been some reason. People are not taken away without any reason whatsoever, and least of all in a country where we are all decent and human.

Looked at from a distance, what is most impressive about our daily life was this miserable happiness tied to the almost total absence of any organized civil resistance or of any form of disobedience. In those countries occupied by the Nazis some form of clandestine resistance developed. Here an utterly disconcerting passivity took over most of society's groups and institutions. The common people, the democratic groups, the respectable institutions had faith, with only small reservations, that legal procedures were being used. Very often they questioned the military, but they accepted the model for the country the military had created.

In this context, let us imagine the immense loneliness of a group of desperate women who one day put kerchiefs on their heads and managed to get the world's attention. This meant transforming anguish into action with a universal voice, a demand not only about the search for their children but for the rights of all human beings. Today we know that those kerchiefs in the street stopped the disappearances and that there are many Argentinians who owe their lives to these Mothers circling the Plaza de Mayo.

Very often people approach these marchers in the circle and ask: "How can you endure it? How can you sleep, how can you eat, how can you manage to go on living?"

This book answers those questions by showing how the mothers have lived and continue to live their daily lives since 1976; how it is that one missing person can occupy a house, the streets, can be glimpsed in strangers' faces and, sometimes, even in a dummy in a store window. And it shows how the silence at night and the meaning in the voices of others can be the same.

The author narrates the journey from loneliness to myth, from the edge of madness to collective consciousness, and she does so by starting with the protagonists' own intimate experiences. And this is their daily life: the waiting and the hopelessness, the photographs in the house and in the plaza, and the perpetual circle around the Plaza of those who have nothing to lose and nothing to gain, but who keep going around because they believe in justice.

Paradoxically, this is not only a book of horror, but also one of strength, of hope, and of heroism. Matilde tells us that in the same way that there are perpetrators and accomplices in the worst crimes, there are also people ready to carry on and to show the best of human nature. In this fight against injustice, there will always be people who make Mariano Moreno's words their own: "There is no surer sign of decadence in a kingdom than when crimes are committed with impunity."

Antonio Elio Brailovsky

THE NEED FOR A BOOK

YOU ASK WHY WE TELL OUR STORY

We were in the basement of the Centro Cultural San Martin with other organizations, selling literature dealing with Human Rights. But we had been assigned a spot where nobody could see us. After exploring a number of possibilities, I discovered a small table on the first floor, almost at the entrance to one of the rooms. I sat myself down there and because a seminar or a meeting on education was about to start, the women came in hurriedly, first buying a periodical, a newsletter or a book dealing with the Mothers. Among the books there were already several titles, most particularly stories or poems about the disappeared children which disconsolate mothers had published as a tribute to their children.

At one point a young woman, an American, approached me. She spoke very poor Spanish, but made herself understood. After greeting me very effusively, she told me that she gave me a hug for all the Mothers in the country, and after handing me a book that she had written, she asked me for one written by the Mothers. After offering her a bunch of publications that she kept rejecting, I understood that what she was looking for really did not exist. And without giving it much thought, I told her that if a book had not yet been written, I would write it.

That providential woman looked at me, smiled and nodded. "Do send me a copy when it is published," and she left me her address. She was the writer, Nam Elssen.

Thus, unexpectedly, the idea as well as the need to conceive a book fixed themselves in my heart, a book which I later nurtured, imagined, how can I explain it?

I MADE THE BOOK LIKE THIS:
SOBBING, CRYING, DREAMING, AH ME
—Alfonsina Storni*

After so many years of pain and heartbreak during which I was only able to talk to myself and cry silently, at last I can let myself go and start writing. I no longer care about my illegible scrawl or my spelling mistakes or about the typewriter I keep from screeching by banging it, and if I put down the word "rancor" I drag the rrrrs until the carriage pushes by me. From this moment on I determined I would no longer talk to myself. I would shout in what I am writing, and my scream would gather strength with every reader that stays with me.

Words used to make me choke up; I had so much to tell, so many emotions, so much pain. So I said to hell with sentence structure but luckily somebody said to me: "Stop, mad woman, nobody is going to understand anything this way!" I answered: "Give me a hand and organize my words to make them fit the syntax, but don't add or take away a word."

With thirty thousand "disappeared" there was no time for syntax. With the slash of a sabre they paralyzed our lives and our culture.

There was no time for a Mother to attend classes: action was needed now.

What use did we have for syntax when every testimony, every "habeas corpus," every letter got only silence for an answer? You don't need syntax for shouting or cursing.

But now we can try to pause and think "syntactically." To recount and to demand.

* Alfonsina Storni (1892-1938): Argentinian poet, newspaperwoman and ardent feminist.

ix

I propose to achieve something that goes beyond my strength. With a scream of rage and rebellion I challenge the prejudiced notion that only those with a university education have the capacity to achieve. I know that I have limitations: I get inhibited, but nevertheless I manage to get my courage back. I challenge anyone who wants to continue a struggle that's worth living for to shed inhibitions and taboos and get out into the street and shout.

I want to write this book so that the next generations can have an exact image of what happened, so that they know us, the Mothers, as if we were their contemporaries. So that they know how we felt and how we lived out this part of Argentina's history, which scarred our families forever. And I also want to write because I have a great need to put myself in contact with other mothers. I don't want to just praise our struggle, I want to tell them where we started and where we came out.

There is a need to divide the waters and to make a chronology of all that happened.

What I would like most is to sit beside you and to tell you everything, just tell you. The book is my effort to sit beside everybody.

At this moment we grieve the loss of many Mothers:

Azucena, Esther, Dora, Mina, Amanda, Lina, Tita...they died in full battle. I remember Esther coming to the Plaza until the last week of her life and Haydee who walked faithfully in the circle with us in spite of the leukemia that was consuming her, and so many others....

When a Mother dies, we don't assume the attitude of hired mourners: we remember her with love, but at the same time, we urge ourselves to go on with what she was doing: searching for her child. There is a tacit rule among us: the best tribute to a sister and friend from the Plaza when she is no longer around is to prime up our spirits so that the circle does not stop—by marching, protesting, or by communicating, as I am trying to do now.

I intend to deliver a kind of account of what we have managed to achieve during these years, starting from nothing, then tracing our route in the march. No, not from nothing: we started out of terror, out of impotence, emptiness, paralysis.... From fog and shadow. Under each kerchief you'll find stubbornness, tenacity, courage, a demand for truth and life. Each mother was at once a strategist and a soldier. That is why I also want this book to be a tribute to the heroism and the affection and tenderness that each of the mothers offered me, sometimes enveloping me in an embrace, other times chiding me when they saw I was down, many other times pointing the way when I could not see it very clearly.

Side by side, we never missed our march in the circle, and from this circle I began to write, out of my small and anonymous place in the struggle.

It did not turn out to be all that easy to gather so many testimonies. I had no professional criteria for choosing them. To speak simply, when I ran into a Mother, I'd propose that we put down all these stories we had to tell.

I found all the stories moving and equally important, and if I have omitted anything, it is in order to avoid unnecessary repetition; but I have respected the way each Mother had to express herself because I know the style of each one very well, and I managed to preserve it. In some cases, I allowed myself to change the organization of the account.

We met, we talked a lot, we told each other things, and then we taped. Many times they would tell me: "Not today, I can't do it today, I don't want to remember. Let's leave it for another day...." Again, sometimes they would warn me: "I will tell you, but I don't want to see that machine. Get it out of my sight!" Not knowing how to proceed, I would hide it between the folds of my skirt and say, "All right, don't look at it. Let's keep on talking...."

A few of the Mothers gave me their testimonies in writing. None of it was easy because while I was gathering the statements, events in the country that affected us kept on happening—happening inexorably. There were moments during which we felt paralyzed, and thus obliged to postpone the task. How many vicissitudes each of us encountered besides!

In spite of everything, with the support of my dear companions, I have been able to accomplish my intended task.

And I don't want to forget our other children. The children who remained.... They suffered immensely...not only anguish for the loss of a brother or sister, but also the human feeling of guilt: Why him while I'm still alive?—the despairing idea that the child spared can see his parents while imagining the hopelessness and need that his disappeared brother or sister must have felt.

Nonetheless, some of us mothers, overcome with despair, were unable to understand their other children's emotional needs.

But at no time did we stop loving them deeply while also fearing for them. However, all our energies, which sometimes hardly seemed sufficient, were concentrated on the search for the missing child. Like in the parable of the prodigal son mentioned by some of the mothers, the absent child claimed our full attention.

That is why I now also feel the need to give tribute to the children who outwardly were not touched or wounded but who suffered a wrenching separation...virtually a loss of identity...who had to live far away, surrounded by smells, colors, and skies foreign to them.

I have reread what I've just written...I close my eyes and I see Graciela's smiling little face. But suddenly she loses her patience: "You, old lady!—what a lot of blah-blah-blah, but you're essentially a goof-off...." At long last, with this effort, I'll try to give a response. A response which strives to be a tribute to you—who were above all a hardworking girl—and to all the children of your generation, who are for us an example of work and devotion.

ARRIVING AT THE PLAZA

One Thursday, during our walk in the circle, I feel the urge to find out what exactly the Plaza had been like in earlier days. So I delve into a fat book of Argentinian history: "The Plaza was always bustling, movement never ceased. Around 1810 neighborhood people would come: children, black women and vendors. They would add to the shouting and the din."* Looking at the illustrations from that time, my own childhood memories of them come alive: countrymen on horseback, poultry vendors, black women selling pastries or sweets, above all the water sellers' carts.

Washerwomen on their way back from the river carrying enormous bundles on their heads. Lots of dogs. And strolling ladies wearing dresses with very wide skirts. By 1844 we can already see the "pyramid"** in the Plaza, a new market, the Government House, the Cabildo's outline, and coaches drawn by four or six horses....

Actually, I always thought of it as a foolish place and to me it still seems so; but not when I find myself there together with the Mothers.

But after so many marches I came to imagine it a small liberated zone separated from the rest of the country. Then I began to discover that it has beautiful trees, and I started to look for some beauty in its two or three standing monuments. On Thursdays when we are there, I love to see the children running, climbing onto the "pyramid".... At that moment I feel as if I were in a very intimate place. We have stepped on

* Ricardo de la Fuente Machain's *La Plaza Trágica*, Municipalidad de la Ciudad de Buenos Aires, 1973. [MM]
** This "pyramid" is actually an obelisk.

each street-tile surrounding the "pyramid" so many times .... Invariably, I ask myself how many miles have we Mothers walked around this monument....

When we are all together, the Plaza is *my* place, it is *our* Plaza, and *all the disappeared are there and everybody is there.*

Moreover, as we Mothers have sometimes commented, it was in this Plaza that the Assembly of 1813 resolved that all instruments of torture had to be burnt: "The use of instruments of torture to get information about crimes is forbidden," and they decreed that "all instruments of torture should be burnt *by the executioner's hands* on May 25 at the Plaza Victoria."*

Over a hundred years later, we stand in horror in this place thinking about our savagely tortured children and their fate.

It is true that we Mothers did not choose the Plaza de Mayo because it is itself a political center or because it is very close to Argentina's great political center, still...how very odd, something like destiny came about, because it is precisely in the Plaza de Mayo that very important events in the life of the country have occurred.

This place, center of celebrations and of rejoicing during colonial times, was also the place where tragic sentences of justice were executed...before everybody's eyes.... It is not mere happenstance either that Garay, the founder of Buenos Aires, had the "Tree of Justice," or "el Rollo," erected nearby. And it is here that we Mothers come every Thursday to demand that justice be done.

The Plaza is a throbbing heart.... It appears to be a spot predestined to be a center of world interest, a window to the world, for half an hour one day a week....

Yesterday I went to the Plaza and I was watching my companions—and everybody else—observing what takes place there, and I insist that at these very moments the Plaza

* Diego Abad de Santillán's *Historia Argentina*, Editora Argentina, Buenos Aires, 1965. [Plaza de Mayo was then called Plaza Victoria.]

is a throbbing heart, perhaps with a touch of tachycardia.... People approach full of curiosity, some from California, others from Australia. One of these foreigners, who could not express himself very well, said something like: "What is it that keeps you in a state of such high emotion besides the suffering, of course? What makes you keep moving?" And I spent the night asking myself that question until I found the answer: the fact that they have eliminated the generation that comes after me, that they have isolated me from the future, that they have separated me completely from my sense of continuity...and that I want to recover it, through Memory.

Without Memory, continuity in life does not exist.

Memory is the well-hidden roots which nourish the flowers with their sap and the fruits that we can see. Without the roots neither the flowers nor the fruits are possible.

I would say that Memory is the root that culminates in the seed which makes the circle of life cycle.

"You have to feel the fire of the desert under the soles of your feet," Rabbi Marshall Meyer used to tell us Mothers.

Memory gives life.

And the Plaza, with all its multitudes, is the perennial Memory of all that has happened since its origin....

> *Everybody leaves their testimony...but the children? Where are they? I miss something ...those children who made me thrill more than I ever had before, who jumped so happily that it looked as if they caused the clouds to run faster.... To see them so united by their songs and catch-words filled me with illusion and brought me closer than ever to a fairer, more human world.... Never in my entire life have I spent such happy hours...of real fellowship.*

That is why when I walk around the Plaza I feel the Plaza asking me: *What has happened? I miss those children.*

Introduction

She introduced me to her daughter
glued on a wall.

"Isn't she beautiful?
She's now 27 years old.
Look at the happy letter
she sent me from Europe
before returning. She's a biochemist.
She's disappeared.
She's been missing for six years.
She's such a graceful girl.
Look at her beautiful handwriting.
From Portugal she sent me this card.
She's a good draftsman.
In this other photo, the one I like best,
you see her sitting in a coffee shop
with her schoolfriends,
She's the one in the middle.
I no longer ask anybody anything.
I just have a dialog with her at night.
Or when I walk along the streets
where she liked to walk.
It's as if she were walking alongside me.
Most often she listens to me in silence
but other times, inside me, she quarrels with me.
But it's good this way.
Then she leaves and I go back home alone
to wait for her.
It's the girl in the photo.
I want to introduce you to her.
Isn't she beautiful?

ELIAHU TOKER

CHAPTER 1

THE CHILDREN

LET THOSE WHO WANT TO HEAR, LISTEN

I take the manuscript to an editor. He rejects it, saying piously, "All the Mothers say the same thing. They nostalgically exalt their children because they are no longer here."

I go back to the street, I walk along staring at the paving stones. How bitter it is, they don't even leave us the right to scream! Perhaps he doesn't know that they were taken away...? They took the best of a generation.... They didn't even let us know why they took them away either, or let us look on at their burial, or give us a place where we could bring a flower...and now they don't even understand that we have a need to remember them, to tell how we remember them.

These children...were they all alike?

Yes: in their interests, their generosity, solidarity, altruism.... Some showed it at student centers, others at the "villas miserias."

They disappeared them precisely because they were doing something.

"All the Mothers say the same thing." I can't get that phrase out of my head. Do all of us Mothers say the same thing? I leaf through all the testimonies. I stop at Carmen Cobo's, from which I take this paragraph. She speaks of her daughter:

"I think that a description of my Inés is almost a copy of those of the other kids because when we Mothers describe their personalities, we can see a common denominator among them: their lack of concern for material possessions and instead their great concern for others, their fellow human beings, their desire for these others not to lack the basic things in the communities where they lived, for fair pay for their work, and, above all, for children not to be denied vital necessities. My daughter especially was horrified by the photographs of the children of Biafra. She belonged to the generation that was moved by those children's real situation and by the Vietnamese War, and by all the horrors that were happening in the world, for she was very sensitive and had a grand concept of justice."

"LET'S JUST TALK ABOUT THE CHILDREN"

When I ask the Mothers to leave testimonies of all these events—history in the making—they all say: "Let's stop talking about the Mothers, because enough has already been said about them. We have to talk about the children themselves."

I keep on thinking that all the talk about the Mothers is continually being used as a media thing by the journalists. In contrast, when it's us who tell about our own experiences, the first thing we describe is our children: how they were, what they dreamt about, what they were fighting for.

When we march and carry the posters with their photographs they seem to be right there, they are above our heads, and we follow them.

One time, at the Plaza, this fellow in a car passed by and shouted at us—trying to ridicule us—"What are you looking for? They're all dead!"

We kept on.

Then Balbín's famous declaration came from Spain stating that all the disappeared were dead.

We kept on.

Alfonsín and his TV images: bulldozers stirring up the bones in graves without names.

We kept on.

And if we kept on it is only because of the quality and character of that younger generation. Only them, since it is their disappearance that motivates this struggle. Only their enormous vitality could provoke a response that started with a walk around a Plaza and finished by becoming a universal scream.

"You feel it, you feel it, the children are present...."
The children are not here, but I still see them
skipping among my flower beds.... But how can this
be, Matilde, how?

"I SAW THEIR PICTURES, THEY WERE SO BEAUTIFUL...WHY WERE THEY TAKEN AWAY FROM US?"
—Sting

To explain that our children are always with us would be to repeat unnecessarily. All of us Mothers feel this way. Ask any of the Mothers in the circle how it is that she feels her child's presence...and she will look at you in astonishment...she will tell you that her child is always there beside her. So, in the very same moment, here in Graciela's photo, and in the very same way, in my heart even without a photo, she is beside me.

Gra is next to my bed anytime I get up; wearing a smile or a serious expression, she tells me: "Put on your slippers, drink a few *mates* and get going: no whining."

Once during Yom Kippur I went to the Temple to listen to the Kol Nidre.... It is music as beautiful as it is profound, and it stirs one's innermost core.... And I was there so absorbed that I could not see what was going on around me...until I came back to myself and I heard Graciela's

3

unmistakable voice: "No Mother...not here, you don't have to look for me here...." And that feeling of vigil—dream-reality—mystery accompanied me for too long a time and made me commit many blunders that only another Mother here or in Chile or in El Salvador could understand.

Graciela's presence is implanted in my conscience. What physical part of my body does it occupy? I cannot tell. With Gra, I discuss, reason, maintain a continuous dialog that for others might be imaginary, but not for me.

I re-encounter her in every setting. Even today, after so many years, the telephone's ring still startles me if it is at the habitual hour when she used to call me from her office. I keep most of her clothes, and in a box I also have some sweaters her grandmother knitted for her, convinced that she would come back.

Gra is present at any family discussion or for any decisions we have to make. She is present in the demands I make on myself to forge ahead and not to give up, in my intense desire to get her back. I also see her enjoying the children of her best-loved friends and the successes of her fellow students.

Gra's presence is in the kids I see running down the stairs as they leave the National High School of Buenos Aires; in the anger I feel at those opportunists who are never absent from political movements; in the worried faces of the people on the street....

For several months I kept going through the same motions. I would get off the bus, and a few yards from the stop I would come to a halt before the window of a boutique. Inside the window three dummies were waiting for me to contemplate them. The one in the middle was seated, and this was the one that attracted me. It was Graciela! How could they have reproduced her face, her eyes, her cheek bones!... And I would stand looking at it fascinated. I wanted to talk to it!...ask her to come back...but her silence was like a hallucination. After a while the owner would come out to

4

look at me with an expression somewhere between curious and hostile. I was bothering her. I was interrupting the free flow of prospective clients.... I could read in her eyes, "move along, move along."

Gra's presence is implicit in all young people's struggles, in all just causes, and in all the battles we have had and will have. In the fury and hopelessness provoked by treachery and submission. But, above all, in all our successes and joys.

And do you know where else I feel Gra's presence? You won't believe it: in some tango or other that moves me.... But also in all the things I am striving to tell.

I used to see them flirting, jumping, running along my paths, playing, demonstrating. Now they come every Thursday, arm in arm with their mothers. When we finish the rite and leave, they stay behind looking on while we move farther away, mingling with the evening shadows, in a grey without hues, waiting for the week that will follow.

We used to go with them to the door: "Be careful. Take your jacket, it's cold!" So we'd watch them leaving, filled with a secret anxiety. They look at us in the same way now when we leave on Thursdays. A silent question is left hanging trembling in the air: Will you come back, Mothers?

Of course we'll come back. Who can doubt it? And I will remain with them. Here they claim the whole world's attention. From these paths in the Plaza, summoned by the presence of these children, the Mothers become the world's moral conscience.

They wanted to bury them in darkness and death, but they could not do it.
They are our light.
And our Life.

They are in unknown graves, but they are much more
than simple memory.
No, they will never be able to erase their names.
Or their wishes for a more just world.
Let the generations that want to hear, listen.
Let those who want justice harvest the message
in their voices.

PLACE

In the morning I go
to a place surrounded by walls.
High grey sad dirty
with posters that say vote for the blue list.
One day I look inside.
It is a shantytown.
People.
More people.
Dressed in cheap cloth
stripped naked of happiness.
A girl offers me lemons
"A hundred pesos a dozen, buy them."
She's thirteen more or less.
My age.
A ruined grocery-store.
filled with rats, with filth,
with deadly germs.
It is a place surrounded by walls
Filthy with human crimes
that are ours alone.

—Franca Jarach

This poem was published in ECO, August 19, 1971. Franca was thirteen
then and was a first year student in the Colegio Nacional of Buenos Aires,
where ECO is published. She was "disappeared" when she was seventeen
years old. [MM]

TESTIMONIES

To the circle, circle,
To the circle, the circle of small leaps,
of songs, of laughter,
the circle, my boy, my girl,
my girl...the circle...
What is its name?

POEMA GARDELLA DE AKERMAN
mother of
LETICIA MABEL AKERMAN
abducted on June 12, 1976, when she was 18 years old

She knew what she wanted

Leticia was rather tall, with olive skin, her eyes were dark, her hair brown and wavy. She had finished high school a few months before they took her away. She completed her five years of study at Normal School # 4 on Rivadavia St. and José María Moreno.

Lety was very well-liked by her fellow students. I believe it was during her fourth year that she started participating in the High School Students' Union.

When I think about Leticia, everything I remember is good, positive; but of course I am partial. I remember something, but I'm not sure whether it's negative. But I do know that sometimes mothers don't like this sort of thing. She was very decisive, firm about what she wanted, and she did not always accept what was asked of her. Because of this she did not agree to stop her activities in the union in spite of the times in which we were living; she considered it to be a just cause. Many times we spoke about this, and I would show her the danger she was exposing herself to by doing anything that could give an excuse for complaint—it didn't matter how innocent it might be—but she would answer with such clear reasoning that she would leave me speechless.

The only argument I had left to convince her was that this movement and everybody in it were doomed and that they were going to pay with their lives in the resulting struggle. And unhappily, this came to pass. Now I only have my remembrances, her smile, her warmth, her sweetness,

8

her beautiful words, her love. I have lost everything. Leticia, hardly eighteen years old, not only finished high school, she was a very hard worker at home; she could do everything and do it well; she knitted, she made her own clothes, she played the piano, she studied drawing, painting and ceramics. I have many of her drawings and sculptures. I think of Lety and I can't understand how they could have dared to kill those kids, those marvelous creatures that took so much work to bring up. Leticia was the youngest of my three daughters. She was ten years younger than Ruth and seven younger than Diana. She was the family's delight and love. Soon after the March 24, 1976 coup, the military unleashed a massive repression, and I started fearing for Leticia: because we knew that just participating in the painting of some collective mural or some student meetings could be a motive for repression. I believe that all the parents of children who were participating in anything experienced the same fear, quite to the contrary of all that has been said about how we parents did not take good care of our children, or that we did not know what they were doing. I knew what my daughter was doing: nothing reprehensible. Furthermore, I considered her concerns healthy and appropriate for her age; at 17 or 18, who does not have a spirit of rebellion when faced with injustice? And Leticia had been breast-fed on the craving for justice.

Her maternal grandparents, a Spanish grandmother and an Italian grandfather, were great fighters for liberty from the beginning of the century. Her paternal grandparents, Jewish, suffered from persecution in Europe; since their youth, her parents had been enrolled in the causes of freedom and justice. Leticia was a product of what she lived, heard, and saw at her home. In spite of what I might have wanted to do to save her, I myself could not have stopped her activities; I had to respect her. The pain of her loss is atrocious, the worst pain a human being can experience, but this suffering is made even greater by its being so

9

unjust. Does teaching one's children love for others, justice, and freedom deserve this reward? Wasn't this the practice of the purest beliefs of Christianity, Judaism, Humanism? The foundation of all religions? The essence of life itself? Once again in history, we have been—she, I myself, and all of us—the victims of the selfish interests which move the world.

Even when we were aware of humanity's bloody history, we did not realize that a new genocide was being gestated. Who could have known at that time about the method of disappearances, of the "sucking in" of people, and of torturing them to death? What mind could possibly have conceived that such atrocities would be used on children, adolescents, on everybody? Who could believe that they would be killed savagely, just like that?

Some of them survived, and thanks to them we and the world know the truth. Leticia was picked up off the street on the morning of June 12, 1976 on the way from Lanus to Lomas de Zamora. She was going with her fellow students to a union meeting at one of the girls' houses; she did not get there or to the meeting. Nine years later, I learnt that they had killed her together with two other kids, 17 and 18 years old, students at the National High School of Buenos Aires. The label on dossier #5038 reads "Triple Homicide in Del Viso;" it took place on July 3, 1976, twenty days after the disappearance, at the intersection between Viamonte and 4th Streets in Del Viso. The neighbors say that they heard cars arriving at dawn, and after that bursts of a machine gun; during the first hours of the morning they found the three murdered youngsters, and they informed the police.

LOLA WEINSCHELBAUM DE RUBINO
mother of
RAQUEL DEL CARMEN RUBINO WEINSCHELBAUM
abducted on June 23, 1976 at the age of 21

Her name will be Raquel del Carmen...

After two boys, an unexpected pregnancy.
"Let's call her Raquel after my mother," I said.
"And Carmen after my grandmother," her father
agreed.
"Why are you looking for girls' names when this generation only produces boys on the maternal side?" put in
an aunt.
"Raquel Carmen doesn't sound good," I kept on
dreaming. "Raquel del Carmen sounds better."
Thus came into being the nominative particle that
would prod her younger brother to call her "del" when he
wanted to make fun of her.
5/10/54: The long-awaited girl is born! What a commo-
tion in the family!
She was beautiful and graceful. A jingle bell that did
not know of gray, intermediary states. Her gaiety was
profound, her sadness was, too. She lived intensely, as if she
had a foreboding about how early she would be cut off.
Mischievous Raquelita. Adventurous Raquelita. Her
father died when she was eight, so my responsibility and
her brothers' increased. And my guilt complexes.... Did we
encourage her social concerns too much?
Would it have been better to have brought them up to
be distrustful, selfish? To have given more value to economic achievements, to prestige?
Did I forget the environment around us? Did I fail to
adapt them to it?

11

We were living in La Lucila between del Libertador Avenue and a high embankment where the train tracks pass towards the Delta station. When that line closed down, the children had a wider world in the direction towards the river.

Those who lived between the embankment and the river were economically more modest. A few owned small horse-drawn carts (typical bottle collectors). Our children exchanged turns on their bicycles for turns on the horse's back.

Raquel: a mixture of daring and of childhood fears.

When going out to the garden in the evenings to feed our "zoo," she would ask me to watch her from the window, but in the light of day, nothing could stop her. She started up acquaintances with unknown people, she would bring home loose, sick, lice-infested animals.

One afternoon we were informed that she was at the police station. That was her first contact with the "Security Forces." Six children between the ages of five and ten had gone into an unoccupied house; the neighbors on hearing noises alerted the police who, with unusual promptness and speed, took away the dangerous, weeping "criminals" in a police van.

Raquel loved to hear episodes from my childhood in the country, our family history. She used to dig around in the past.

Raquel's forebears

In a town in Old Castilla, Anastasio Carrasco was conscripted for the colonial army in South America. Like many others, once here, he started a family.

A native of Andalucia, a nobleman, he made his family with a native woman whose last name was Rojas. According to comments made in the family, there was some Indian blood running through her veins.

Some of the descendants from these Spanish branches intermarried with settlers of Italian origins. (Grandfather Rubino used to say of Raquel: "How Italian she is!")

The Weinschelbaums, horse-merchants in the Ukraine, together with many others from the same area, started their trip towards South America in the ship, Weser. They were the first settlers in Moisesville.

Raquel grows...

From the blending of all these branches of immigrants Raquel, the Argentinian, was born; if she did not get the honor of raising the school flag, when she got home later she would ask me to watch her while she solemnly pulled the curtain cords. If I was busy, she would place the cats on the sofa as spectators.

Her childhood was happy in spite of her father's absence; her brothers and relatives tried to compensate for that.

Her adolescence was happy too, because in this society, physical beauty is a quality that instills certain security in its women when it goes together with a lively natural temperament.

Dances and boyfriends would follow.

But also other concerns. She saw that all of us were working. She too: from the time she was fifteen she tutored private grammar school students from the lower grades. Nevertheless our education allowed us to live in moderate circumstances.

The injustice she saw in everyday life and all around her shook her.

She was part of a generation more moved than others by what was taking place around them.

She found out that poverty isn't what those unfamiliar with it believe: just a matter of buying less. No, poverty is a tin roof full of holes over a room shared by parents and children alike, the surrounding mud, water in a far away faucet, an ill-smelling toilet, scabies, lice, permanent insecurity—an inheritance transmitted through generations of people who in childhood don't get adequate nutrition, a perpetual confrontation with an incomprehensibly coded world.

Raquel's Sundays no longer consisted of dances and movies.

She would come back with her friends with calluses on her hands, lice, and a big smile. She wasn't doing "charity." These kids had used the knowledge their privileged position had given them to work together in mutual respect to improve the miserable conditions of life in the shantytowns. They dug drainage outlets, they cleared brush, and they shared *mates*.

Having been brought up in a provincial family, the vocabulary, expressions and some of the customs she met were not foreign to her. She delighted in the *criollos*, the solidarity they practiced without attention to theories, how they took care of each other's children when need be, the way they shared their homes and scarce food.

What these Sundays shared with her previous ones were the gatherings around the guitar—but these people had not received any academic instruction; she gave them her first guitar and then lent them her second, a better one. During one of their searches, the police took away those two "dangerous weapons."

March 1976

A Union meeting called by the teachers of San Isidro's primary school at School #1. For the first time high school

14

teachers were participating. It was a triumph for us. We worked out due-dates for many projects. But we would quietly say to each other: before which of these short-term deadlines (let's not talk about long-term) will we hear the sounds of the boots and the tanks?

We laughed because until then, in spite of how bad the military coups had been, we could not imagine what would unfold on the following day, March 25, 1976.

MARÍA ADELA GARD DE ANTOKOLETZ
mother of
DANIEL VICTOR ANTOKOLETZ
39 years old, abducted on November 10, 1976

"We are wasting time," said Azucena Villaflor de Devicenti. "What we have to do is to go to the Plaza de Mayo—meet there. When there are enough of us, we'll cross the Plaza, then go across the street, and we'll get ourselves into the Government House, because we're not going to let anybody stop us, and we're going to talk to Videla...." I always remember Azucena's words. You ask me for my testimony. I'll start at the beginning.

I was born in San Nicolás de los Arroyos in the bosom of a family deeply rooted in the city. I grew up surrounded by love and devotion; I was protected and educated. I am speaking of seventy-five years ago. The city's daughters had no possibilities then other than graduating as teachers. After that my older brother gets sick and we move to Córdoba where I get married.

After getting married I live in foreign countries— always in America, where I learn or where, or to put it better, I develop something that I always had inside myself: pain when I saw injustice, and the wish, almost the need, to serve others, or at least in some imperfect way to do something. Well, the years go by, I have two children: Daniel, a boy, and María Adela, a girl. But time accentuates differences in character, morals, conduct, the way people act, in such a way that makes it impossible for me to continue family life together with my husband. And I get a divorce, returning to Argentina where with my family's help, I finish bringing up my children, who follow the careers for which they felt called. Daniel graduates as a lawyer. He gets a doctorate specializing in Public International law. He is above all a researcher in law. My relationship with him was always cordial, understanding. I love my children dearly, I am always busy doing things for them like every other mother, as is natural, especially at the time I am referring to.—What do I want for them? I want them to have a profession in something progressive that will give them security.

Daniel went to high school at the Colegio Nacional in San Nicolás, the only one there at that time, and then he continued his studies at the Catholic University in Buenos Aires.

An option that life keeps offering us

I want to tell you what my son was like, to paint a portrait of Daniel as he was.

He was generous, a tireless reader, impatient, had a great sense of humor. He studied Law, got brilliant marks. He got invited to teach international law as a teaching assistant while he was studying; later on was an adjunct instructor at the University of Social Studies, which was later dismantled, and at the University of Belgrano as well; he competed and won a position teaching the sociology of international relations at the National University in Buenos Aires; he was Head of Studies and Research at the Institute of Public Law at the University of Belgrano's Law School and Associate Professor at the same school from 1971; also Chief of Studies at the Mar del Plata Catholic University; and again Associate Professor at Buenos Aires University's Law School. He also worked privately in his profession, accepting the defense of some political prisoners. He traveled to Chile twice in 1974; where he managed to save and bring back several Argentinians who had been abducted by Pinochet's dictatorship. In 1973; when there was the possibility for a democratic resolution of Argentina's problems, he was appointed Chief of Cabinet by the Secretary of Foreign Relations, Juan Carlos Puig. He worked at this job with great enthusiasm. Three months later Cámpora's government came to an end. Right-wing Peronism took control, and under its compliant protection and cooperation the activities of the Triple A (Alianza Anticomunista Argentina) kept increasing until it ended up by consuming the right wing.

Actually, until Daniel had found his own way, his route had been harsh and painful. During his adolescence, his intelligence and surprising sophistication hadn't allowed him to easily accept the old-fashioned teaching at his high school. Nevertheless, he respected the good teachers, even venerated them. The humanistic and professional education given by the Catholic University shapes two contradictory attitudes: one is traditional and individualistic; the other, by way of reaction, is an option that life itself keeps offering us: the democratic, popular, and cooperative. This road, paved with insecurity and misgivings, is the one that Daniel took.

During his fourteen years as a professor, Daniel finds himself rejected by those whose class interests he threatened. But without any restrictions whatsoever on his time, he dedicates himself to student groups and the door to his house is permanently open...until the fateful morning of November 1976 when six armed men in the name of the

United Armed Forces burst into his house to kidnap him and his wife, Liliana Andres, who reappeared a week later.

To go back to his career: Belgrano University, which was daily more and more selective and ideologically more and more anti-popular, no longer wanted Daniel in its classrooms: they fired him. The University of Buenos Aires School of Sociology—where the teaching staff now accepted the presence of a policeman in every classroom—found Daniel's commitment unacceptably disruptive: he had to resign...and from the Law School as well. So his opportunities kept disappearing as the space for democracy kept narrowing. With the end of Cámpora's government and the advance of the repressive right came the end of Daniel's hopes.

His defense of political prisoners in Argentina and in Chile, among them the Uruguayan Senator Enrique Erro; his exhaustive report to the Third Congress of the Argentine Association of International Law on the increase of violations of the right to asylum; his repeated denunciations of the harsh conditions in the prisons and of the general lack of respect for human rights in Argentina, are aspects of his long search for justice so long in coming and still delayed. And he never made use of violence or encouraged anybody to make use of it. He fought with legal and political weapons but with growing intensity against the institutionalized violence. After the March 1976 military coup, Daniel kept on defending political prisoners, with all the risk that this entailed. That is why they had to silence him, to shut him up; that is why the dictatorship had to kidnap him, that is why he is one more of those tens of thousands detained-disappeared in Argentina under the military governments that followed after 1976 That is why the whole family (María Adela no longer can contain a long and painful bout of crying) keeps on looking for him, as we have been doing since the first day and as we will keep on doing always—seeking to vindicate our absent son whose crime was to fight so that his country could have democracy and justice.

Azucena's words

When we came painfully out of the stupor, the horrible surprise, the disorientation caused by Daniel and Liliana's disappearance, we sought out every possible legal avenue to find out where Daniel was, and so created strength out of our weakness. We Mothers started to get to know each other during our anguished walks. The Mothers, who suffered identical situations, got to know each others' faces without knowing each others' names. And one day in April 1977; at a military chaplain's house belonging to the Navy, a spy priest received us and pretended to be interested in us, and got out of us every possible bit of information concerning each of our families. I am talking about Emilio Grasselli. This was in the neighborhood of the Stella Maris Church. That day, one of the Mothers (Azucena) said that we were wasting our time listening to this man and going to police stations and military chaplains and command posts and even by making all the inquiries each one of us was making.

Poor us. We did not realize the truth of the situation, the "why" of the disappearances, the fact that the main responsibility fell on Videla and his cronies: that it was necessary to silence the voices of the dissidents in order to establish a specific economic policy—under the fateful doctrine of national security—that would completely hand over the country, that would bury us in this external debt from which not even our great-grandchildren will be able to dig their way out. Our naivete at that moment was such that we believed we were going to sensitize Videla!

In April, 1977; when we were marching towards the Plaza de Mayo, I told Bousquet: "At 5 o'clock we are going to demonstrate at the Plaza de Mayo, across from the presidential palace, so that at long last Videla will have to agree to give proper attention to the cases of our disappeared children."* As you can see, I could not imagine then that the dictator, Videla, was one of the main people responsible for the disappearances.

And thus, impelled by Azucena's words, which forged our way, and headed by Azucena, on April 30, 1977; we fourteen Mothers met at the Plaza full of trepidation. What action were the fourteen of us going to take at the Plaza? Absolutely none.... But we were tenacious, and kept on going Thursday after Thursday. We did not ask anybody about their ideas, or "what their children had been involved in," or about their family's ideology. The fact of having a disappeared person, that alone, created a sisterhood among us.

* María Adela is "Marta" in Jean Pierre Bousquet's *Las Locas de la Plaza de Mayo*; Fundación para la Democracia Argentina: El Cid Editor. 1983.

LIDIA MIY URANGA DE ALMEIDA
mother of
ALEJANDRO MARTÍN ALMEIDA
20 years old, abducted on June 17, 1975

We are at the Plaza, someone takes my arm. We look at each other and smile. It's Tati. She tells me: "I want to give you my testimony too, so that everybody knows what my son was like." It didn't take Tati long to hand me what follows:

It is so difficult to synthesize everything that I feel and I think, I miss and I grieve for my dear Alejo. It is such a deep pain, so far inside me, so many tears shed...sometimes I scream out of control, bordering on madness...other

20

times I am silent, swallow my bitterness, but I will never be resigned. Never.

I was telling you the other day that because of my upbringing, my family, my social background, I was not only anti-Peronist, but "mea culpa," I was actually for the armed forces, how awful! How could I have been? And to think that there are still those who continue to be, against everybody's interests.

I remember how Alejandro—reflecting his natural disposition, so warm and understanding—would hug me tight and between laughter and kisses would say: "Ah! My little militarist, my dear, crappy militarist; but just the same, you're what I love most of all."

I also remember how on his birthday he would give me the gift of a flower along with a card that said: "Thank you, Mom." My God, he was always a song to life! To this life that he loved, that he shared, the life that they wrenched away in such a merciless and criminal way....

I would like to write many other things that I hold fresh in my memory, but I can't now. I want to, but I can't. My emotions are too strong. If just remembering him...but I have these poems from Alejandro. I'll let him continue....

FRIEND

I would have preferred
that the beauty of your face
were in what you thought
and felt.
Then it would not matter to me
if your thoughts and feelings
were like your face.
I prefer women
with faces like nothing
I prefer those who carry
their beauty inside them.

CHAPTER 2

THE MOTHERS CONFRONT
THE DISAPPEARANCES

In my hands I lift a storm
of stones, rays and strident axes
thirsty for catastrophes and starving.
I want to dig the dirt with my teeth,
I want to separate the dirt bit by bit
in dry, hot bites.
I want to mine the dirt until I find you
and kiss your noble skull
and ungag you and bring you back.

from "Elegy" by Miguel Hernández

I WANT TO MINE THE EARTH
UNTIL I FIND YOU

Prado Museum, 1969: Around that year, the room of Goya's black paintings was opened, Goya only. There was a painting that attracted me: "The Wedding," but notwithstanding, there was another which would remain engraved in my memory: an enormous monster devouring his own son whole.

Many times I've related this painting to the horrors we have lived through in our country: a terrorist state that ingested its own children.

Enormous, like Goya's monster, who takes the child by his waist with the utmost ease—it's the way they carried off our children—they were utterly defenseless.

I AM LOOKING FOR MY DAUGHTER
AND I STILL WEEP.

I remember my mother's death. It was many years ago, a long agony, very, very slow. I know almost everything about my mother's life and all about her death, especially her death, because I stayed at her side so long...including her wake. I could not part from the coffin in which she was laid, so that my sisters, already grown-up women and filled with anguish, would ask me to touch her, to make sure that she was really cold. And I am telling all this because—how absurd!—I have

25

lived with my own daughter, but I am ignorant of everything about her death, including what happened between her disappearance and her final destiny. In contrast, about my mother's childhood I know very little, because she didn't use to talk about it. About Graciela's life, of course, I know everything, with its ups and downs, but—what became of her from the time of her abduction until her death? Even today, I don't have a reliable official version about what they did with my daughter. What I think happened is only intuition.

I have also come to imagine—to intuit—how Graciela's last moments were, what she could have felt. We know from the testimonies many of the Mothers have heard that some prisoners were totally ignorant of their oncoming fate. I don't know why, but I sense that my Graciela perceived when she was going to be eliminated. One afternoon I felt...something that Gra must have felt...something that submerged me in an infinite sadness, in the certainty that she was going to be wrenched away from everything that she eagerly wanted to see again, from everything she loved. I imagine that very swiftly the images of her loved ones, companions, friends, loves, passed through her mind like lightning, and to each of them she said goodbye with an infinite bitterness, and I think she must have told them: "We shall never see each other again."

HOW CAN WE EXPLAIN THE DIFFERENCE BETWEEN DEATH AND DISAPPEARANCE?

I know it perfectly well, I feel it, I live it, but I cannot describe it. We must not forget that it is not a common situation, not a norm. It is different...we are not prepared for it: not even the Bible mentions such a possibility or its response to it...maybe the Cain-Abel case, when God asks: Where is your brother?

A disappearance places you in a very large, dense cloud from which you cannot escape, because in the unconscious a hope always survives, while you can rationally assume the absoluteness of death. The truth is that from the first days of Alfonsín's government, when the news that there were people alive started circulating, the whole group's determination was energized and renewed. Everyone thought: "Perhaps mine is alive."

When we deal with the death of a loved one, even if it is violent or premature, we accompany that loved one to his burial, looking for consolation in memories, shared experiences, accompanying all this with pre-established rites lodged in the unconscious, until the figure starts to become blurred.

When we deal with one of the disappeared, an unknown, culturally uncharted relationship is established. The disappeared person himself agonizes in his impotence, with the conviction that his life will be totally erased from the face of the earth, that nobody else will know about him. In the same way, his mother lives out the agony of uncertainty; she cannot prevent her thoughts from accompanying the disappeared at all times: in the darkness, in the hunger, sickness, torture, in his call for his mother, in the filth, and in the humiliation; and in death, in the decomposition of this well-loved matter, in the rotting of his bones.

When a person dies, his survivors know the story in all its details and colors: they can tell and describe chronologically all that happened until the final end. Everything is known. And there is the need for the survivors to describe and to listen to all those details over and over again.

When someone disappears by force, everything remains surrounded with a tangle of conjectures, indeterminacies, doubts.

Every member of the family who receives the news constructs his own account, but the fate of the disappeared is condemned to be an eternal mystery. The survivors become victims of terrible emotional changes, because the information becomes distorted with disinformation, the truth with lies, ignorance, doubts, and the hope of life: the disappeared is continually buried and unearthed—and all this over a period of more than twelve years! There is no authority either during the "proceso" (the name given to the dictatorship's program) or the so-called democratic government that followed, which will assume the responsibility of calling the parents and telling them at what moment the murder took place, and explaining the motive for it. Even men who were elected by popular vote make themselves accomplices to the mystery, to the illegality.

Lost in my own questions, which do not give me one peaceful moment, I meet Emilio Mignone. I believe that he must have a concrete and detailed answer. Here are his thoughts:

> *"Desolation and impotence. A situation which is totally different from death's presence: death is predictable...if it is natural and even if it is accidental. But disappearance not due to a catastrophe— be it an earthquake, a flood, a shipwreck. A premeditated disappearance because a group of individuals—because a system—decides that a person is to be abducted, without giving any news about his or her existence, is something new, disastrous, and incredible. That time passes is beside the point. In spite of the fact that because of my profession (I am a lawyer) I see cruel and criminal situations, I never could have imagined this."*

I looked for a word that could express my feelings, and could not find it. "I miss Graciela," but the verb "to miss" suggests nothing to me. The Spanish dictionary does not have a word to express my feeling of horror and perplexity. The image of the person forced to disappear does not exist in the Argentinian Code of Justice, nor does the punishment for the person who caused it.

I am looking for a word that would synthesize our state of mind, one which, what's more, does not exclude a feeling of perplexity. Well, in the meantime I repeat to myself over and over again "morriña," "morriña." I savor it because, when I voice it, I half-close my eyes and compress my lips, feeling a slight tickling in my throat, as if I were about to say, "Mother.".. Mother and death...do I want to die...? I mustn't. Nostalgia also touches me deeply. I will go on looking for that word.

Ah, Graciela, all this seems to me like an unbelievable nightmare. Your father and I trying to find an explanation for the inexplicable, to write about the terrible experiences we have lived through on the verge of old age, surrounded by memories.... And thus, without intending it, I feel you are so near me that when I turn around, I hear your breathing. I feel that you are encouraging me with a smile...giving me courage so that I dare to go on.

You are here, right here with me, stretching the upper part of your body to see what I am writing, and smiling to give me courage. Well then, dictate something. How can I go on? Frankly, I'm afraid.

I am living with a double image in a double space, a double life in a double dimension.

I don't know what else to do to find you. And I don't want to lose your image: I'm not dreaming, I know I am wide awake. How can this happen? It's better that we part company, because both of us cannot be present here at this moment.

I am afraid to turn around. I am afraid to look at you; but if you are not here, how am I going to survive?

I remain staring at the paper: I don't understand anything, but something has just happened to me.

I come to myself, I leave the typewriter; luckily, over my head upstairs there are a series of noises. I know it's my neighbor's grandson. I'm glad that he pulls me out of this state. I will try to get up and do something.

One of those senseless things that I have to do daily.

There is something even more horrible than all of this: how I reacted—by shaking off your warm and precious presence...how could they...how could they...?

Nothing gives me consolation now because you are not here. Those months during which I carried you in my body are left behind, far behind. Left behind also is that sweet memory of the emotion I felt after your birth, and when I held you in my arms for the first time. How could I have given birth to something so beautiful, so sweet? Maybe... some of that memory is already a bit blurred. I am not looking for my baby, what I am looking for is for that girl who came back to me after her adolescence came to an end, who turned into my friend; that woman who suffered, laughed, was afraid and who then won out, that girl who could not leave in my arms her own image in the form of a child, that woman who unknowingly gave me a new life, wrenching out of me a personality I was unaware of.

TESTIMONIES

To the circle, circle....
I look at you who look at me,
who might want to know,
and I, from my awful clarity,
I, from my insomnia
will ask you
if you have any children....

ELIDA BUSI DE GALLETTI
mother of
LILIANA GALLETTI
31 years old, abducted June 13, 1977

"You, who do you have that's disappeared?"
Those words felt like a bucketful of water, but at the
same time I understood that I was not alone....

Each of us, when touched by this misfortune, must have
had his or her own reaction. I can tell you that we didn't
have the strength to go out immediately. We stayed in the
house. I remember when they told us that they had taken
Liliana...we were literally knocked to the floor, and in that
condition we flailed about in each other's arms, Alfredo
and I, covering our mouths, pressing them against the
floor, because it was less than a month since we had moved
into this house. Before then we had lived in La Plata. So we
were afraid that the neighbors would hear us. It was
terrible, we could not understand what was happening to
us....

Well, all we could think of was a very dear friend who
was an army man. And we went walking, holding on tightly
to each other from Rivadavia and Medrano Streets, where
we lived, to Belgrano, where he lived. We didn't find
anybody, so we left our friend a small message. But we were
not able to go back home to sleep. We rented a little room
in a hotel on Avenue de Mayo.

On the following morning, we went back home and
waited for him; when he arrived he told us, "I won't
promise you anything, I'd already warned those children
that we could see this coming, but we'll try to find out
something about them." And so it was. After four or five

days he brought us some news that left us so hopeful.... "I asked and they gave me this answer: Yes, this individual is alive, but please, don't ever ask questions again, because if you do, there will be problems for you."

For us this was like the certainty of Liliana's life for ever...it was hope. Nevertheless, at this point, in spite of the fact that the disappearances had been happening for over a year (they had taken Lilianita away in June, 1977), we—and I believe many others—kept on thinking that the disappeared were alive, that we were going to get them back....

We were unable to remain at home, we went to live with some friends. We must have stayed with them for about a month when we started to ask for information, like everybody else. We sought the help of Mr. Marino, a La Plata lawyer, who had an office here in Buenos Aires. The first thing he asked us was: "Did you present a "habeas corpus?" and Alfredo told him we hadn't.... Imagine what idiots the situation must have made of us, Alfredo being a lawyer and not to have thought of that!

Well, Mr. Marino presented the "habeas corpus." He presented it and furthermore he signed it at a time when nobody, but nobody else would have signed it. Most lawyers did not make themselves available to take those steps. He is a very honest man, very sensitive to people's problems. I recall a remark made to him by the Secretary of the Court when we went to present the habeas corpus. Marino was offended by it and utterly disgusted, so he answered: "What I am doing is perfectly correct, and I will do again and again, as many times as may be necessary." And he remained our shoulder to cry on. Alfredo and I kept going to his place and he kept on trying to get us more information. He knew a person who was very loyal to him because he had gotten his son back, and he could always ask for his help. For a year they gave us data about Liliana's being alive. It might have been true...it might not have been.... Very often Alfredo and I would think it over and we would tell ourselves: Couldn't Marino be telling us this so that we don't die of a broken heart?

Marino himself asked us—he was a member of the Permanent Assembly for Human Rights: "Did you go to the Assembly to make your accusation?" So after so many tumbles we began to enter into this reality. And we went to make our report to the Assembly. And also to the Argentinian League for Human Rights.

During these first months, we would sit at the table but we could not eat. Eating would have been like giving ourselves a gift to which we had no right...what was our daughter eating? What could have become of her? We had to find out about her, and how to get her back.

I am telling you so that you can see the state we were in. They took Lilianita on June 13, and her birthday is September 5. On that day I made her a cake and my sister came to spend the day with us. I made the cake...well, because perhaps she would be coming.... And after my sister left, do you know what I did? I cut a slice of the cake, and because I had been told that they were taking many of the disappeared to one of the Army facilities over in Palermo, I thought that my daughter might be there. And I went and I unwrapped the cake and turned it into crumbs at the foot of a tree because I thought that perhaps Liliana might have been looking through a window at the trees.... I think it was madness, something that doesn't make any sense.... Later on, I learnt that all of us were doing senseless things. Every one of us.

At that time, we didn't know what to do about the house. You can imagine that since we had moved in only a month before, the house was in complete disorder. But who felt like starting to organize things? We would go out into the street, we would walk, go into a cafe to eat, just anything...always thinking about what else we could do.... One day, at the Assembly, they asked me: "Do you know that the Mothers are getting together?" Then I went to the

Plaza, but I went at around 5 p.m. only because that was the time it occurred to me to go. I thought that after leaving their jobs, the Mothers went to the Plaza. I did not find anybody, nobody could tell me anything. I went again: nothing.

Then I went back to the Assembly and asked for information and there they told me that they went on Thursday afternoons, early.

When I got there I saw a small group. There must have been some twenty or twenty-five women. They were not yet wearing white kerchiefs. And I could see that they were moving, that they were talking, it looked like a beehive. But I did not dare to approach them.... This group...you didn't know if they wanted to allow you to come close, I said to myself. And I went back home.

The second time I went to the Plaza, I sat down on the same bench...it was during a period when I used to cry all day long until I didn't have any more tears. A woman sat down next to me and I don't know why, both of us must have had the intuition that we had similar concerns. She sat down and said to me: "Have you gotten near them?" And she looked over to where the Mothers were. Then I asked her: "Do you have a member of your family who's been taken away?" (I wasn't yet using the word "disappeared"). And she answered: "Yes, but I'm afraid to get near them... they seem so sure of themselves." "Me too," I said. But finally I made the decision and approached them. Nobody paid the slightest attention to me, I felt they were an already established clan, like a group of people who knew each other. And I was there, a poor little thing, who didn't know what to do.... I left again. The following week I returned once more to the Plaza and with more determination I got in among the Mothers.

At which point, somebody asked me: "Who do you have that's disappeared?" That word felt like a bucket of cold water, but at the same time I understood that I was

35

not alone, that we all were going through the same thing. And they started to tell me truly terrible things. Some of them had seen their children tortured before their eyes—in their very houses—before being carried away. Others had lost two or three children...it was horrible. And so I started going every week, I started entering that world, and I was accepted in the same way that all of us who approached were accepted. And I remain branded, and tied forever to the struggle and the objectives of the Mothers.

Never, never did they ask us anything at all as we walked in our circle, except our names, not even our last names.

How alike the four of us looked...

Both Alfredo and I are clearly of Italian descent. My four grandparents were Italian. Father was a carpenter. I am the elder daughter and the one who studied. At home studying was much encouraged. I became a history teacher and had the pleasure of teaching in the same high school from which I graduated, the La Plata Liceo. First I was a teacher and later vice-principal. I had already had my two children. Lilianita was still attending grade school and Hugo had started high school at the Colegio Nacional. Lilianita was a brilliant student, very gifted, with a strong capacity for reasoning. But what was most important to her was the fact that she had been chosen year after year, in both the grammar and high schools, as the best fellow student. And she really was that. Besides, she had common sense and a clear political vision, which I lacked. I used to ask for her advice when I had a problem to solve. So between my children and my husband, who was passionate about studying the political sciences, I got help in under-standing something that to me had never been very important in my life. Later, reality made me take a different path.... My husband also had three grandparents and parents who are Italian. But while I came from a plain immigrant family, Galleti's father was a professional. He was a lawyer, so that he came to Argentina for different reasons, and, as it happened to many, he met here his Anita, got married and stayed in the country.

Alfredo was very jovial. At lunchtime or dinner he used to describe to the children episodes from history or geographical curiosities, always in entertaining, accessible ways, but also in great depth.

Left alone after Liliana was abducted and my son was forced into exile, we used to comment on the many beautiful memories we had and ask why life should have struck us with this misfortune...? But we were not the only Argentinians so touched, we were two among many.... And so we come to understand this, because we remained together, and, besides, many human rights movements have grown: at the student centers of secondary schools and universities, in the unions. All this shows that the Argentinian people have started to become conscious of the tragedy that the country is living through.

Now I don't even have Alfredo to remember things with. You know that Alfredo died tragically, by his own choice. Though I can never admit that it was something he did, after much thought, I believe he was in a deep decline. He was suffering from a great depression and I am sure that what sunk him deeper were the terrible, tragic films...I don't understand how they could do it...when they opened the graves without names, which all the cemeteries are plagued with, and they showed them on TV. They heaved them into the air with bulldozers.... Look, it's something that causes—I don't know what to tell you, nausea, desperation...but how could they do it in that way...? My husband had glued himself to the TV, something he never liked, he never watched. And I believe that this somewhat determined his action, and so he took his life....

37

It was Liliana—the same dear face that I had never seen before in any of my dreams—

I have to start by selecting memories about Liliana because I am used to thinking about her, her companionship, and also Alfredo's, during all the lonely moments in my life, when I do nothing but think about things.

I remember how she loved to sing, especially tangos. She had the whole collection of them in her head because her memory was excellent, and she also had a passion for horoscopes. Her father would cater to all his "little girl's" tastes and as soon as the year's first horoscope came out, he would bring it to her as a gift; he would also buy her anthologies of tangos. But Liliana could not sing in tune, so since everybody laughed at her a lot (it didn't inhibit her, she had a great sense of humor), she defended herself by saying that it was her own singing style and so it had to be acknowledged.

You can take it as a mother's vanity if you wish, it does not make me ashamed, it really gave me great pleasure: Liliana got a prize from the Academy of Historical Sciences. This prize was a gold medal for the best biennial graduate in History. Our daughter was the recipient at the University of La Plata. But when she received the notification, Liliana became uneasy, because all these personal academic rewards did not sit well with her. They seemed to her mere formalities. And she asked her father to represent her and to thank them in her name. She found it wrong to make distinctions among the students. She believed that each person should be valued for giving the best they were able to offer.

Liliana chose history as her career because she thought that through the study of Argentina's history she could also analyze its social economy, in which she had become quite interested. There is, as a matter of fact, a booklet put out by Centro Editor. It was prepared by her and two other students, about the birth of the Argentinian oligarchic class in the year 1860. And she also has a study of the beginnings of journalism in our country, a collaborative work with the professor whom she assisted.

At the end of 1976, she had gone to the Permanent Assembly for Human Rights because of the human rights problems. Liliana was writing reports for a group of people that were to form the Argentine Commission on Human Rights. These reports were sent to other countries. Liliana was pretty, very lovely, short and somewhat thin, but not really skinny. Her hair, which was straight, needed a lot of care, so when it became a bit greasy she would say: "My spaghetti noodles are ready." Her eyes were beautiful. I used to say that her eyes were honey colored because they matched her hair. She always had a ready smile, she really enjoyed a joke. She was extroverted and needed to have people around to talk to. She always had things to tell. I don't want to leave my son out. Hugo was also a wonderful kid, but right now the main characters in all this are the disappeared children, right? Because they have taken with them the mystery of their end, what their last moments were like. One might lose a child tragically in an accident, a disease, but we know absolutely nothing about what happened to the disappeared; we couldn't give them our help if they were sick or weak....

I did hear something about what could have been Liliana's last day, but it was just conjecture, nothing else.... Her fate is a permanent question mark. I believe I will die with it.

Through the National Commission on Missing Persons (CONADEP) I heard about another girl who had been taken to the "pozo de Banfield" (the Banfield well), one of the many places of detention. My daughter was among the people mentioned as having been seen there. Just this year I was able to see this girl. She came to my house on September 4 (Liliana's birthday is September 5). This girl, whose name is also Liliana, arrived at the "pozo de Banfield" on

September 7. They had brought her from other places blindfolded and they threw her into a cubicle and asked her: "Are you Liliana Sambrano?" She answered "yes" and then they asked if she had attended the University of La Plata. The girl nodded affirmatively and they left her there with the order not to take off her blindfold.

Next she heard somebody knocking on the wall with her knuckles, and calling her by her name. She answered and she heard:

"Listen, put your ear to the wall and listen to me carefully: I am Liliana Galletti, from Humanities too, do you know me?"

"No, I don't know you, but I have heard about you a lot."

"At the University they always called me 'the Italian.'"

"Yes, yes, yes, I've heard of you."

"Listen, relax, because when they bring us here it means they're going to question us. Then we're placed under the authority of the Executive Power, so take it easy."

At that moment she heard the guards bringing in food and telling the group behind the wall: "Don't eat a lot because today you're going to travel." And a few hours later she heard a lot of people walking next door, something like twenty people being taken away.... Look, that was on September 7...

Well, she and I looked at each other and the girl held my hands. We didn't know what to say. Finally, I asked her: "What did you think, the worst? Don't worry, tell me, you get so hardened by this...."

Then she nodded affirmatively and told me that two hours later they sent her to clean the rooms which had been vacated; they had been told to leave their clothes and all the clothes were there, folded.

From that moment on I began to think that September 7, two days after her birthday, could have been Liliana's last day.... But what happened to her? Which of all the horrible

40

things described? Which one befell her? Did they throw her from a plane? Did they shoot her? What really horrifies me is thinking about the ovens, that really overwhelms me....

I was so out of my mind...and the mystery still disturbs me.... Look, I remember something odd now that happened to me.... I believe it was in April or May. I was sleeping. It had begun to get lighter and suddenly I heard Liliana's voice calling me: "Mom, Mom!" And then I looked—already half-awake, I began to see an angel, but an enormous angel! It was Liliana. Her dear face was just the same, like it had never been in any other dream.... And I was saying: "But what are you doing up there, Lilianita, come down...." And while I was saying this, she kept on ascending, passed through the ceiling and left me.... And I, who am not a believer, I always thought that it was like a story...one of those dreams...how do we call them... premonitions.

In spite of these two stories I am telling you, none of us thought that our children were dead before the OAS came, but that's no longer the case. This was true to such a degree that when Alfonsín assumed power, we believed that there had to be many concentration camps in the southern part of the country. Our children would have to be alive there, and we hoped and we believed, that was the reason for our euphoria, that's why we were on the streets, so full of energy. When fifteen, then twenty days went by without our receiving any news, our last hope vanished. And then we decided that we had to continue our fight, but we had to know what had happened to them, because each day we had to convince ourselves that they would never return....

Like almost all the other Mothers, I got used to looking at our child's photograph every night before going to sleep. Alfredo had her picture on his night table too. And I started looking at all the photos of her that I had. And to group them together, and how strange, looking at them I discovered that Liliana's eyes did not sparkle. They weren't

the laughing eyes she always had permanently ready. I
found sadness in the depth of her eyes. That worried me
for a long time, I don't know if deep down she didn't have a
melancholy soul....

Sometimes I feel that I should ask Hugo's forgiveness....

Sometimes I feel that I should ask Hugo's forgiveness,
because when I talk so much about Liliana, as I'm doing
now, I don't know, poor dear...not as much now, anymore,
because he's already a grown man, but perhaps when this
misfortune occurred, he might have felt that both Alfredo
and I were devoting ourselves entirely to Liliana. And we
were not able to realize that he was also suffering from all
this horror. Hugo had to go into exile after the police
raided our house, when all of us, Alfredo, Hugo and I were
removed from our jobs. We had to make a decision, and he
decided that he had to leave the country. We had also
thought that Liliana had to go, but, unluckily, too late. And
poor Hugo, before a year abroad was over, he found out
from a friend that Liliana had disappeared. At the beginning, we were unable to talk to him, because we were crazy
with desperation. I believe that three days later I gathered
the strength to call him.

The dictatorship destroyed our family. It took my
daughter, my husband too, whom I also lost in the process. And my son is abroad. I have to manage by myself,
churning around these thoughts which are my permanent,
day-long companions....

At this moment, I am thinking of recovering my
strength in order to fully rejoin the fight, the work we have
been involved in during these last ten years.

You must understand that this new intensification of uneasiness is tightly related to the recent passing of the law of *punto final.*

Note: Elida Bussi de Galletti died in September 1990 without seeing her testimony in print. [MM]

ESTHER ARACELA LADO DE SANCHEZ
mother of
ENRIQUE SANCHEZ
21 years old, abducted in 1975

Before his disappearance, my son had been unjustly jailed. The director of the jail and everyone else said that he was a good kid, very good. I came back home and started asking questions, because I didn't understand anything: if he was so good, why did they put him in jail?

God, I beg you: protect him and grant me the certainty that I will get back my son alive. A young worker came to me one day and said: "I told my foreman that I have a friend whose heart is as big as the world."

My son was unjustly imprisoned...they took him on January 21 and they discharged him in 1975, free of any charge and he disappeared three months after having been let go, because during that time they let prisoners go in order to kill them. So I began to be afraid. They called me on the phone and they asked me if I knew anything about my son. And I said that I didn't.

I saw him on a Saturday at noon. That was the last time I saw him. I was very nervous, I had a premonition something ugly was going to happen. But we had lunch together and then, as always, we danced the Emperor Waltz. Ever since he was a little boy he liked to dance with me, without

43

any music. All of a sudden, he stopped eating and said: "Mom, let's dance." And we danced the Emperor Waltz. But the last thing I could have imagined is that at that moment I was saying goodbye to my son. And that was the last time I saw him. And after that I had no information, absolutely nothing, nothing.

I knew a police inspector and I immediately called him on the phone and I told him that my son had disappeared and that I thought it had something to do with the people burnt out in Flores. Then he called the police station in Flores, but they told him that there wasn't any one there like the person I had described. Then I went to the morgue, where the bodies of the victims of the fire were. And my daughter and son-in-law went in with dental charts, and my daughter told me: "he's not here." But I wasn't satisfied. The morgue had me obsessed. I would go there and grab hold of the bars. And then I got hold of a doctor who identifies bodies when they are burnt in airplanes. With the dental chart in his hand, he told me: "Señora, don't look for him here, because he isn't here." But until I came upon somebody competent who could identify the bodies there, I kept on going back. And the morgue-keeper told me: "Señora, I'm telling you the truth. I want you to find him here because I'm afraid you're going to go nuts. But if they tell you he isn't here, he isn't here." But I did not know where to turn.

A terrible vision

I have to make clear that what I am describing about the people burnt to ashes at Flores was what appeared in the newspapers. And when I went to the morgue, there were many burnt bodies. It was something horrendous, macabre. I thought that my son was among them. Of these, there were four in a large vat, completely burnt up. From there, I started looking all over. And I ended up by going to the Government House. And I went to the Ministry of the Interior's office, where they showed me the folder with the names of those who had disappeared, but my son was not mentioned. And they told me: "Señora, maybe he will never reappear." I couldn't make any sense of that. Why wouldn't my son reappear? In spite of the fact that they told me he was not in the morgue, when the bodies were removed, I went out of my mind, I wanted the body, I desperately wanted a body.... When they took them to the cemetery, I went and I asked the keeper: "Where are the bodies burnt up at Flores?" "Look," he told me "all of those are the ones burnt up."

I was carrying an enormous bouquet of gladiolas. It was very windy. I thought I was in another world. On each unnamed grave I stuck a gladiola. I thought that I would be able to sense which one was my son but the dirt did not send any signs to me. And I kept setting out gladiolas. There was one gladiola on each grave. If I succeeded in leaving one for my son I'm not aware of it. But I left one gladiola on each unmarked grave. And as I was leaving, I told myself: it looks like a garden. All of a sudden I thought it was a garden, but immediately I asked myself, what lies there underneath? What sadness! My God, my God! And I was unable to leave the cemetery. I grabbed hold of a tree. I was crying so hard I could not leave, I could not walk until I poured myself out, screaming, and I began to walk, to walk until I left the cemetery.

You tell me I am an intuitive person, do you want me to tell you about it? The day my son disappeared, I had a dream: I did not see my son, but I did see that two shots were fired and that a car was set on fire: in the dream I saw that the fire caught fast, as if everything were burning, the whole car burnt up.

It was a terrible vision... As you can see, I was in bad shape. I was going to a psychiatrist who found me to be very disoriented and who advised me to go to the Argentinian League for Human Rights. There they would direct me. That is how for the first time my son appeared on a list as one of the disappeared. Then I met one of the Mothers who had known him when he was in prison, and she told me to come to the Plaza on such and such a day. I don't remember the date very well, but we were very few Mothers then, and I started to attend. I believe there must have been some sixteen Mothers. Each time more and more Mothers joined us because they were killing more and more people. More people were disappearing. At that time they didn't say "killed," at that time they said he or she disappeared: was he killed? Do they have him? Where is he? Where isn't he?

I didn't want to go even crazier.

When I go to the Plaza, I go full of love, with great respect for the Mothers, who are suffering. And so, one day, I asked a Mother: "Why are you crying? How long is it that your child is missing?" She told me: "Six months." And what could I say when it's three years! "And when did your son disappear?" she asked me. "At the time of the Flores conflagration." And it was at this time that I felt the certainty that he might still be alive because this woman told me: "Your son was not there because one of them was identified, and then three women and someone else who was from Entre Rios." Then I remembered that it was on a Saturday morning that they grabbed those people, and the hope that my son could be alive returned again. And I kept on going to the Plaza hoping to find him, and I kept on looking, like all the other Mothers were. Now, what I did not do was to go to the Government Ministries because I did not like the game they were playing with us. I knew they were lying to the Mothers. They had them come just

46

in order not to tell them anything. They would tell them to wait sixty days and then sixty days more. It's been a torture that the military and the employees, those who killed them, and those who didn't kill them, used on us. It was a horrible psychological torture. I did not want to have anything to do with it because I did not want to go even crazier.

That's why when Yolanda said to me: "I'm going to give you an address, write it down." And she told me: "You have to be at such-and-such a time at the Plaza de Mayo." And I started going, but going like a soldier goes to battle, without really knowing what it was that I was going to face, but I met the Mothers. We were all suffering the same pain. But I did not weaken, I kept on. And then I loved to go, I felt relieved. It meant meeting with people you could talk to. Because I can tell you that I had kept the fact that my son was one of the disappeared well-hidden. The only people I could talk to and talk at ease with were the Mothers. There was close companionship. I especially remember Yolanda, who is a very devoted Peronist. One time she told me...can I tell you what she told me? I had a photo taken with Alfonsín, and she said to me: "Get out of here with that guy, you'll see how he's going to shit on you." And now, when I see her, I tell her: "Even if you're a Peronist, I love you, I'm very fond of you." "I love you too, but tell me the truth: did he or didn't he shit on you?" And I answered her: "No, because he didn't kill my kid, or any of the other kids, and he's going to do what he can, even though you don't believe it. I believe in him, he's going to do what he can...." And Yolanda said: "He didn't get us back even one of our children."

Listen, when Alfonsín assumed power I was at the Plaza. And I felt as if something was exploding inside me, I felt democracy like a surge of energy! How strong it made me feel!

Ah! And I asked Yolanda when they started killing the kids because they are always saying that it was in 1976. My

47

son was disappeared together with many others during the Peronist government. That's something everybody forgets. This thing did not start in 1976. It was in 1974 when kids, about whom nothing has ever been found out, started to disappear.

I felt very good in the Mothers' company, and when we'd go to the demonstrations, and there were so many, oh, so very many!—I used to shout so much, so much! My arms would hurt from lifting them to shout. But, what can I tell you? So many years have gone by—twelve—that I can no longer shout. I don't any longer have the strength I used to have.

But I will keep on going. I keep on going even if I can't shout, I keep on going. I cannot shout, but I feel inside me a burst of strength because we must find the justice that will give us peace. So that it allows us to sleep, so that we may depart in peace. Because what we need is to have peace, we need to be told what happened to our children.

I have written something about this, so that they know everything, everything that happened. Of each missing individual, they know the story, they know what they have done, they know where they were thrown, they know how they killed them. And they must tell us. We are not going to stop until they tell us about our children's fate, even if it is about their bones. I want his bones, but the bones they know are his. I want them to tell me: I killed him, or I burnt him, or I reduced him to ashes. But I want that person to tell me: your son's bones or ashes are in such and such a place. But he has to start from the beginning, I must know who took him away. I have had always the idea in my mind that I really want to know who abducted him, why they abducted him, who gave the order, who gave the order! How I would like to know who gave the order!

Ah! You know what I want to tell you? Christmas for me is bad. Ever since I was a child, it's always been bad for me. I remember now that one year, on New Year's Eve, the human rights organization sent out cards with the picture of a gathered family, toasting, not in happiness, but toasting. They kept on living, but there was an empty chair. And the empty chair stood out. Yes, the empty chair is noticeable, even when you are surrounded by champagne or cider bottles. The absent child is absent, and he causes us to be absent as well....

CHAPTER 3

THE SEARCH AND THE WAIT

We still sing, we still ask
We still dream, we still wait
In spite of the blows aimed at our lives
by the resourcefulness of hatred
that banished our loved ones to oblivion

Make them tell us where they have hidden
the flowers
that used to adorn the streets
living out a destiny
Where, where, have they gone

—Victor Heredia

LET THEM GIVE US HOPE...

When we still had lots of hope, but were simultaneously growing exhausted by the authorities' silences and their brutal indifference, what did all the years of searching and waiting mean to us fathers, mothers, brothers?

The abduction and the disappearance of a loved one from our homes obliged us to change our way of life, our habits, our social and family customs, from one day to the next. We were quickly displaced and marginalized.

We became desperate: imploring street-wanderers, beggars. A tiny bit of information, that's all we wanted. But the regime humiliated us, more than anything else, it humiliated us.

Just a five word sentence, "There must be someone alive," gave us motivation for long conjectures, speculations, and polemics. And it would not fail to energize us anew.

How could they put up with us?

We were supposed to keep our mouths shut: we made accusations.

We were supposed to be submissive: we unmasked them.

We supposed to be quiet: we screamed with all our might.

They needed to bury things quietly: we dug them up.

Above all, we were supposed to stay very quietly at home: but we went out, walked around, got into unimagined places. Some of the Mothers went as far as the centers of government and public institutions of Europe and the United States; others traversed streets, neighborhoods, towns.

WE WERE ALWAYS READY AND WAITING, WHATEVER THE TIME, DAY OR NIGHT

And in the meantime, every Mother lovingly awaited her child's return, keeping all of his things in familiar order just as they had been left, and always ready to receive him at any time of the day or the night.

In the small shanty in the village where she lived, Marta kept the special corner tidy where her son slept; he had been drafted. His bed was always neatly made, and on it some freshly ironed shirts. Just like his Sunday suit, perfectly hung on a chair.

Sarita had bought a good quality suitcase and she had it all ready for travel with shirts, pants, shoes, and a new leather jacket—even her son's books—because she thought that were he to be freed, it would be best to have his things ready so he could leave the country immediately.

Another Mother used to tell how she always kept a tin full of her disappeared daughter's favorite biscuits ready. She would constantly replenish them, so that at any moment, when her daughter returned, she would find fresh ones.

And as to myself, what did I do?

A LETTER, IF I RECEIVED A LETTER....

When I met Angela Westerkamp, a great friendship developed spontaneously.

She was awfully anxious about her son, who had been imprisoned.

There were periods of great danger, especially for young people who were in jail and who had been condemned by judges who were accomplices of the dictatorship. When the repression started to loosen up a bit, Angela got into the habit of phoning me whenever she got a letter from her

Gustavo. He would write from jail, maybe from Rawson or some other penal institution.

This became a ritual full of emotion. I would leave everything I was doing and would run to Angela's house; I would ask if I could prepare myself some *mate*. And I would tell her: "Wait, wait until I make myself comfortable." And then the reading of the long-awaited letter would begin. Angela would read slowly; the letters arrived censored, but nevertheless they would bring a lot of information. When we didn't understand a word, we would figure it out between the two of us.

At this time I imagined that I also would shortly receive letters from my daughter. To receive and read Gustavo's letters was like a preview of something I intensely wanted to take place. I'd dream that soon I would know where they were holding Graciela...this never happened, but I will never forget the deep emotional effect those letters had on me.

BETWEEN HISTORY AND TALES

We Mothers had to learn lots of things. Even today, a group of my companions attend history classes regularly. They want to know the motives, real and political, that have led to such fateful circumstances as the ones with which they have been involved.

At the beginning I would read, devour everything that I thought would shed a bit of light on the disappearances. At that time, everybody was reading the novel, *Roots*. I got very interested in the subject. It told of how a human group was abducted from someplace in Africa in order to be enslaved, how they were transported by boat, about the suffering they underwent in the hands of the slave traffickers, and about the codes the prisoners devised so as to communicate among themselves.

I would read all this with very great interest while I tried to imagine the condition of our children. At that point the only thing we knew is that they were being subjected to torture.

I also learned something about economics, and I understood that the disappearances had a lot to do with the dictatorship's project to subject the country to total foreign dependency. And I learnt that the methods of repression were learnt at a school in Panama.

After searching and searching, a history about the prisoners in the German concentration camps fell into my hands: a very strong bond was forged among them, as if they formed part of a new family after each of them had lost his own. Upon reading this, I thought that our disappeared were in solitude, in darkness, but also forming a family to support each other.

"DO YOU KNOW WHY I TALK TO MYSELF?"

My whole life turned into continuous walking, searching, and inquiring. And when I walked alone on the street and saw the faces of all those people indifferent to my misfortune, who appeared to be so far removed from what I was going through, I would ask myself how they could live and be happy. Didn't they know that many, many kids had been abducted? I believe that I talked to myself. No, I am sure that many times I talked to myself as I walked. Once at siesta time, I was wandering along a solitary city street, I was looking at the sidewalk tiles, I believe I was counting them; the street was deserted. An older man, well-dressed, passed me by. He looked at me, laughed, and kept on walking. And I kept on counting the tiles. But suddenly I was overcome by a fiery indignation, something I could not control. Immediately I hurried on and reached him. I touched his shoulder and I

55

said to him: "Sir, you went by me and you laughed, right?" "No, no, Señora." And I insisted: "Yes, you laughed because I was talking to myself." Then, truly amused, he said to me: "It looked as if you were happy, right?" And without letting him go on, I shouted: "No, I'm not happy. Do you know why I'm talking to myself? Because you have to know that there are lots of people disappearing. And I'm the mother of a girl who has disappeared, and I no longer have anybody to talk to about it. That's why I talk to the stones in the street...."

The man's response was to turn as pale as a piece of paper, stutter and attempt to apologize. I realized that I had distressed him deeply, but my indignation had been so great that I left him with his apology unsaid and ran away.

I would say that every day during those sad years of searching, all of us Mothers experienced that type of episode, or other ones even more disagreeable.

WHEN WE ARGENTINIANS WERE "UPRIGHT AND HUMAN"

We Mothers all had to deal with running counter to Argentinian society during the 1978 World Soccer Championship when the whole country was one big party even though the abductions had not stopped.

Who paid any attention to us during this time even though we were looking for our children without knowing whether they were alive or dead?

We simply could not understand their unbounded happiness while we were undergoing so much, our whole world spinning around the search for one person, trying to find out what had they done with her, trying to get some news, the tiniest bit of news. You put your whole heart into that, all your soul, your life went into that.

But we knew that the Military Junta had gone all out to change the world's image of the country with this championship. Blue and white flyers appeared everywhere before the tourists' eyes, stuck onto shops and car windows, from which they sarcastically spat at us: "We Argentinians are upright and human."

SADNESS...ENCOUNTERS... MISENCOUNTERS....

Our relationship with our other children was not easy. Determined to find our missing children, we did not realize that we were abandoning the ones who remained at our sides—and how they suffered! Nevertheless, I know some Mothers that had the ability to devote themselves to the search without neglecting their emotional relationships with the rest of their families. In other cases, what happened is that they felt pressured by their children's attitudes. The children tried to make them stay at home, afraid their health would break down. Then the Mothers would pretend not to have the absent child on their minds, thus avoiding discussions, minimizing the comments, the pain, the anguish.

Generally, it was a somewhat tense situation, when it was not one of outright family discord. Verbal encounters and confrontations colored even more dramatically the endless days of the dictatorship.

And how the members of the family who had to go into exile suffered! Only they can know how much. The torture of hiding their identities, the longing for their immediate families and childhood haunts, the idea that perhaps at that very moment some information about their beloved siblings had surfaced in their country at a time when they had to be so far away.

Once I was told of a plane returning to Buenos Aires. An exile's wife was planning to return to see her dying father. The news spread like wildfire among the Argentinian exiles in Spain. At the airport on the day of departure, a group of young people met who simply wanted to be near somebody who was going to step once more on their native soil. They hugged and touched the privileged individual who was able to go home even in such a transitory way. The possibility of just a single person going back sharpened their sense of being in exile. They were condemned to remain there, anchored, until who knows when, dispossessed from the color of their own sky, from the pattern of the streets in their cities, from their smells, their music.

And they watched the plane depart. It disappeared into the sky. And the sky of their hopes swallowed up that machine, which was the only thing that joined them to their world. The smell of gasoline and the infernal noise of the motor remained in their stomachs and ears until they went home, where all their pillows gathered their nightmares and their uncontainable tears.

HOW ALONE WE WERE!

A short time after Graciela was abducted, her brother left for exile, he as well as thousands upon thousands of Argentinians. Thus they fractured a generation. Detained, disappeared, prisoners in inhuman conditions and emigrants abandoning their country. Really, the country was abandoning them. Those who remained behind were also in a state of disappearance, albeit without being physically absent, because they could not talk, or, unsurprisingly enough, give their opinions or meet, for that would have meant the end of their lives.

We were left all alone. Hardly had Gra disappeared, when my son left; but a short time later I received a very small silver-colored metal box. Inside the little box was a message of love asking me to open the box whenever I had the need to be with him.

So I walked along the streets with the mystery of my daughter's fate pounding in my temples, with the box tightly held in my closed fist, and wrapped in a heavy cloak of oppression: a cloak knit on a weft of pain, of death, of suffocating anxiety, of loneliness, of fear. And in that weft, there was a tenuous, very thin thread of hope.

A GRANDMOTHER'S LONG WAIT

If only Bobe, my mother, were alive! I can see her at the Plaza—always the first one there and talking to everybody because she was so restless. And she would always have something to argue about. She walked along with me shouting and declaiming—but now she was dead! What could she do? She had an option! To put herself into a dream of the other grandmother during a siesta!! This poor woman woke up very worried, but intrigued: "I dreamt about Bobe Ana, it was as if she were right here. She was very worried about the children and kept telling me: 'The kinder, the grandchildren.'" It looks as if my mother had transmitted some of her unease to her. I didn't like that dream at all, but I tried not to give it any serious thought. "It's nothing but a dream," I told myself. Ten days later, Graciela was abducted.

How did the other grandmother react? She hung Graciela's photograph facing her bed, so that she could look at it constantly—every night and every morning when she got up. It was her silent vigil and hope. Gra, her eldest granddaughter. She was her pride and joy. "When we have her back—because surely she'll turn up in some jail, the same as so many others have—I'm going to visit her, wherever she is, even if I can't get my shoes on, I'll wear my slippers I want to see her so much."

Every afternoon, grandmother Ida would sit in the same armchair, constantly knitting, above all for the grand-daughter they'd taken away. "How could they have taken her away like that, without letting us know where they've got her, whether she's alive or dead?" In a box which she especially asked me for, she kept accumulating the results of her knitting, which she kept for Graciela's sake when she came back.

She always had an enormous ball of wool yarn on her knees. Very slowly, she would use it up.

A gray cat would curl up next to the yarn. She unstintingly gave it all her affection in spite of the fact that it was a street foundling, a plain, rickety little animal. I would look at them and suspect that grandmother believed this cat had the soul of a saint or was somebody else's reincarnation. But I never dared to ask her.

I could not start to tell her all the events that took place on the street or all the organizations I was active in. Everything was incredibly horrifying and wretched: deaths, abductions, and more deaths.

Sometimes, the two of us would listen to the radio or read the newspaper. Grandmother began to discover a different kind of language that would make her uneasy: confrontations, raids, subversive, stateless, atheist, Marxist, knocked down.... I knew other words which did not appear in journalistic lingo: hood, parsley, sucking center...which I chose not to mention to her.

Little by little, grandmother's hope began to fade away, the same as her existence.

LOOKING BEYOND

Confronted with a lack of news, in my desperation I started seeking out fortune-tellers. I looked for them all over the place and finally got to Utrecht, Holland, where there was a very famous one.

I met him at his own house. He was a very nice person. Through his interpreter, Mrs. Marjolyn, I told him that I was

60

looking for my daughter and that I did not know whether she was alive or dead. Looking at a map of Argentina, he then told me that she was alive but that he could not detect where in the country she was. This produced in me a tremendous feeling of joy and consolation. I cannot forget it. (I learnt afterwards that many people from our country consulted him about their disappeared children.) While he was examining the map, he would trace different points in our geography with a pencil until he stopped at Buenos Aires. Then, with the pencil he traced some streets. Afterwards, by poking and checking, I came to understand from his description that these corresponded to the place where Juan B. Justo and Rivadavia Streets meet. A long time afterwards, I learnt that there had been a clandestine center of detention operating in that area.

Looking for Graciela, looking for my daughter, I have truly done things that during my normal life would have seemed to me the actions of someone demented. This man I've been talking about was a very famous person because he had pointed to the place in the Andes where some Uruguayan kid had suffered a plane crash.

I consulted him one or two more times and he always insisted that Graciela was alive.

IN THE NEIGHBORHOODS OF MY CITY

Something that I put into practice several times was to take a bus, any bus—for instance, maybe #100—and to go as far as the suburb of Lanus. The madness of sitting at a table, a table by the window of a coffee house, asking for a cup of tea, but not drinking it, simply waiting for somebody to go by! Graciela had so many fellow students and friends in Buenos Aires that I imagined that some of them were going to pass by there. And they would recognize me and then we could talk about Graciela and do some conjecturing. I simply longed for an exchange of notions. Of course, nobody ever got close, or recognized me.

This is the way the Mothers' days went by, so long and overwhelming, but we never yielded even one minute to the silence and the marginalization they wanted to impose on us.

TESTIMONIES

The circle in silence, slow, concentrated,
we, the women in dark clothes,
with dark looks,
the women who walk in the circle,
myself a woman, myself a mother,
in Adriana's name,
in Pablo's name,
in Raquel's name,
for my son, for my daughter....

CARMEN ROBLES DE ZURITA
the mother of
NESTOR JUAN AGUSTÍN ZURITA
abducted at the age of 25, August 1, 1975 and of
MARÍA ROSA ZURITA
abducted at the age of 21, November 1, 1975

What weapons are you talking about?

I am going to start by telling you about the abduction. It
was on August 1, 1975 at two o'clock in the morning. They
came in by smashing down the large front gate and pro-
ceeded to smash down all the other doors standing in their
way. My son was in his bedroom of course—in his under-
wear. By the time I got up to answer and open the door, the
men were already inside because by then they had knocked
the door down. All of them were armed, all of them were
wearing masks, and they ordered me to give them the
weapons and asked me for Juan Zurita.

These men confronted me and asked me for the
weapons, so I told them: "Me? Weapons? What weapons are
you talking about? I have two bicycles here—the ones the
kids use to collect the newspapers and then take them to
the vending places, those are the weapons I have, I don't
have any other weapons."

Then they locked us up in the room where I slept with
my girl and they went into action in my son's bedroom.
When I realized that they had taken him away, I saw at the
same time that they had torn all the mattresses. All of them
were perforated. I came out and asked this guy where my
kid was and where they had taken him because I wanted to
give him his shoes and his clothes so he could get dressed.
Then the guy tells me that it wasn't necessary, that he'd be
back immediately. And eleven years have gone by and soon

it's going to be twelve. I have gone through all the procedures, as we all have done. Because we have searched high and low in this country, we have gone abroad, we have complained to the Church, which is the party that's given us fewer answers than anybody else: they have never contacted us about anything, nobody has concerned himself about these cases, not in Tucumán City, nor anywhere else.

In Tucumán City very little, and even less in the small towns; at least here in the capital there is somebody who's been moved...at least surreptitiously...by so much suffering...who told us something, although he too was risking his head. And it should be very clear that those men of the Church who put themselves out for all those in pain also had their heads chopped off, like Monsignor Angelelli and a few others.

My son was an ordinary kid, like any other kid, but he would come and talk about the needs of others.

That was his politics: other people's needs. He hurt for those who didn't have enough, for anyone who needed to buy medicine. He would put himself in his place and say: "Well, I'm going to do it, I'm going to look for it and I am going to take it to that poor guy...." He would fight even with me...now I understand what he was telling me. I would ask him: "And so, are you going?" "Yes, I'm going," he'd say, and well, when we calmed down, he'd start talking: "And so, what do you want? They're so ignorant that—you know what they do? They go and buy wine and some salami and they get drunk, and that's because of ignorance, Mom," he'd tell me. "And how are you going to cure it?" "It's difficult, because those men on top—they don't want to cure this, because the greater the need is, the more servants there are...and you go and you talk to those poor guys, it's as if you threw stones at them, because they're so ignorant that they can't understand, so you figure it out: they live in a one-room hut and they have ten children...."

65

Sometimes I would ask him: "Juancito, what did you do with the shirt I bought you fifteen days ago?" He'd answer: "Look, I gave it to someone who didn't have any." My son was one of those people who'd go without eating bread so I could give it to you, so that you'd give it to somebody else's son who didn't have any, that sort of a kid. And since such people should not be walking around loose, their heads have to be cut off, because other people—what they want least is that there should be people like this.

My son was a skinny kid, one of those kids who...how can I say it?...like the king of the birds...everybody liked him: and where is that skinny kid now? What's become of that skinny kid? Where is he? Because everybody loved him. He was a kid without any vices, a hard-working kid who helped me with my work because I had to work so they could study, because I had nothing. Look, I had to work in my kiosk, selling newspapers, magazines. That was my work and their work. He would finish with that and would leave because he worked at an electric plant—he wasn't one of those boys who'd spend nights out, passing the time. He was a hard-working kid like any other.

I'll go on telling you about the abduction. On that same day I went out ready to fight for him. I went out immediately to question one person after another. We got connected with Pisarello, a defender of political prisoners and he told us: "Well, look dear, you have to leave, because there's no other alternative, dear, because they're going to take you too." And me, with this idea that you didn't believe in anything because you couldn't believe in anything...the only thing you believed was that, yes, you were going to find your son. Then Pisarello was abducted, they took him away too, dear; it didn't look like an abduction, he was taken from his house in a gentle way, his wife told me afterwards. They allowed him to put on his shoes, they allowed him to get dressed and they took him away. After fifteen days he reappeared—those who saw him told me—

66

in a bag, cut up with a saw, his eyes jabbed out.... Well, when that happened, I told myself I'd better run because if they did that to him, why wouldn't they do something worse to me? Then I came to Buenos Aires without knowing anything about anything. I didn't know anybody, they had already taken my girl too, they took her after my son, ninety days later. When they took her, I went immediately to talk to Pisarello, and he told me: "Look, do you know why they've done this to you? The girl doesn't have anything to do with this, the girl is innocent, but they have taken her because you stirred up things for them every hour of the day and night—what they've done to you is their revenge. There are those who could be witnesses for the girl, but who'd offer to be a witness? Nobody, because nobody wants to talk, they're all blind, they're all dumb."

My son was taken with another kid whose name is Roberto, who is also one of the disappeared; there are lots of disappeared during that period, 1975.

Look, I didn't mention the children's names: Nestor Juan Agustín Zurita, my son, who was abducted at dawn on August 1st, 1975...because my son didn't "disappear," my son was taken...and my daughter, María Rosa Zurita, they took her ninety days later. And up until today they are still disappeared. All these cases happened in the city of Tucumán, in that same capital city of the province.

Yes, I did get the habeas corpus, like everybody else. When they answered you, if they answered you, they said they didn't know. In Tucumán, everything was no.

The Church didn't answer. I wrote outside the country, I wrote to the Pope, who never answered, though he knew better than anybody else, and maybe was satisfied with this genocide being carried out. Because everything was looked upon favorably by them, because if they had not looked on things favorably, those bums in the military wouldn't have done anything and things wouldn't have gone so far.

They've gotten to the point they have with the complicity of the Head of the Church.

I came here since I could no longer do anything and they had murdered my lawyer, who was more or less in charge of my papers and who had already warned me about what could happen to me when that really terrible thing happened to him. I got myself a job as a sleep-in maid. I didn't do anything but go around in circles. Well, those times went by until I was able to establish myself a bit and get connected with the Mothers, but dear, it was tough going. During that time I didn't have a thing, because I didn't know anybody. The Mothers helped me a bit and found a place for me to work; they gave me a hand.

I did any kind of work to eat until—I don't know why—somebody said to me, why don't you buy yourself a bit of land and I got myself this plot with some pesos that I had left, dear, for which today I thank God, who gave me the courage and the will power to build this roof, and now I'm living in my own place. And I have to give thanks every day while I am alive to those who have backed me, to those who have given me loans, to those who have trusted me. And I built my little house, and that's where I'm living now.

To me your daughter is my daughter.

But without forgetting what has already happened, I keep on looking for my children and everybody else's children, because to me your daughter is my daughter, she's a little bit mine. My children are a little bit yours, because I hope yours will appear so that she can tell me, so I can find some consolation, know, know what happened to some of them...because the children belong to everyone, to every person in those circles we walk in.... Ten years have gone by already since we started these circles. Sometimes I don't know why we keep marching in them, because nobody listens to us. The policies of Alfonsín's government promised so many things.... And now three years have gone by and nobody tells us anything.

When the civilian government came to power, didn't you have hopes? But how could we not be hopeful? It wasn't me alone who was hopeful, all of us were hopeful. It's time for the constitutional government to make use of its weapons because they have promised us so many things...they've promised the country so many things, and it has not fulfilled even one of them. I want somebody to tell me which of their promises they have fulfilled.

But it was everybody's illusion. Not just my hope, it was the country's hope: that the disappeared would reappear, that Alfonsín was going to give an answer, that he was going to tell the Mothers about the children, that there was going to be justice. But what answer did he give us? NONE.

In spite of everything, I am going to keep on asking for justice, I am going to keep on marching, because I want to know who is the guy who gave the order, who pulled the trigger, and where...and where they threw the bones, of each and every one of the disappeared. Of each and every one of the disappeared! Because I am not interested in what some people say: that my son was a guerrilla. Because it's a lie, because they yanked my child out of my house, they stole him from my own house, so nobody can say that my son was in the mountains. And they came and dragged my daughter out of her workplace because I stirred things up every single day, and they didn't like that and they had to do something or other to shut me up.

I now feel calm because I have my own place to live in, a house that's mine, and a job. I can escape sometimes to Tucumán to see my sons, the two of them who stayed there, and my two daughters as well.

All of them are all right, thank God. I have a daughter who's a doctor, but she doesn't work because what they pay her is hardly anything. I go there, my grandchildren are all happy, the older one is now nine years old and didn't know anything about things, but now he knows because his parents told him what happened to his aunt, what happened to his uncle; so he asks me things like: "Why did they do it? Who did it? Why did they do that to my uncle? Why did they do that to my aunt?" Because they had a big photo made and they told the children: "This was your uncle, some bad men came and took him from his house." Then he says to me: "Grandma, if I knew who took him away, who did that to him, I don't know what I'd do to that guy." He's a child barely ten years old, but he already has the notion—in his very veins—that he isn't sure what he'd do to that insolent scum who took it upon himself to barge into other people's homes, to knock down other people's doors, to steal people.

FANNY BRENER DE BENDERSKY
the mother of
DANIEL BENDERSKY
abducted when 26 years old, September 16, 1978

Daniel asks them if they have a search warrant

In 1976, my son Daniel finishes his career in physics and starts working for the Atomic Commission at the constituent army post, where he involves himself with his own project. Now concerning his disappearance, it's a bit tangled up with his failure to get a job appointment. Because he disappears just when he was involved in some work at the Commission which would allow him to obtain a graduate degree. At that time, because his work was highly respected, Dr. González, his boss, suggests he should apply for an appointment. Daniel starts the procedures and, of course, at that time everything went through the SIDE (Servicio de Informaciones del Estado) to get his personal and political background. And it comes to pass that they reject his appointment. This was on Thursday, the 14th. And when his boss calls him with the news, Daniel goes to his house immediately to see him. There they decide to go to the Commission on the following day to see the Director of Human Resources, Engineer Vasalla, and they agree, with another Director, to see a general and find a solution to the problem of his former political activities, which were not very serious, but just the normal things that college students do. That was on September 15, and they agree to meet on the following Monday so as to take the necessary steps. On Saturday, September 16 at 11:30 there is a knock at the door.

On that day at our house we had bought an organ and we had planned a meeting with a group of fellow students, cousins, personal friends of the family, to give a sort of concert for somebody in the Castro family. So the house was ready for a meeting, filled with lots of emotion, lots of enthusiasm...and at 11:30 the doorman rings the bell. I open the door and he tells me: "Señora, there are some men here who want to talk to you." Then one of them steps forward and tells me: "Federal Police." And four fellows come forward in a very unthreatening way, without any visible weapons. Daniel was playing the organ, practicing for that evening. The men tell me to call him. I go to look for him and when we return they give him the order: "Identify yourself." When I return with his documents they tell me that they are going to search the house. Then Daniel asks them if they have a search warrant, and one of them tells him that they have no need for it because they're from the Federal Police. Two of them go with Daniel to his room,

71

one comes with me and the other one remains as a guard, let's say, because he goes back and forth from one place to the other. They don't search Daniel's room, they don't remove anything, they just allow him to get dressed; suddenly I see that Daniel is changing clothes and I ask him: "What's the matter?" And he answers that he's going to be interrogated and that he'll be back in the afternoon. They didn't search my room either, actually they didn't touch anything. And when they were about to take Daniel away, I tell them: "I would like to accompany him." And they answer: "But of course, accompany him." Then Daniel tells them that we want a witness to the operation who can tell my husband when he returns home. And they let me go in search of the doorman. When I return with him, I see that they are already leaving with Daniel and I ask them: "But how come? You're already taking him?" And they tell me: "Yes, just go and turn off the gas." One of them follows me, but when I turn off the gas on the stove and I turn around, the one who was accompanying me is no longer there.

Afterwards, I find out from the neighbors that they came in two cars, a red Peugeot and I don't remember the other kind. Four men came in, but a few more had stayed downstairs.

I wasn't thinking during those moments. I was so blind, I couldn't understand anything. But the moment he disappeared I got an idea. I ran to the grocery store to ask for money to take a taxi. I was so beside myself that I couldn't remember where I had put my wallet. I couldn't see it, but they hadn't taken it away. So I ran to ask the grocer for money.

I took a taxi and rushed to my sisters' house; they weren't there, so I rushed to my brother's to see what could be done. Meanwhile I was alone. My husband had gone to our weekend house in San Miguel. Then I went to my sister-in-law's, and from there we called Dr. Mignone, who told us he'd see us at four in the afternoon. In the meantime I had gotten hold of my husband. So José came back and we went to Mignone's house. In the midst of all this, then, I had the pleasure of meeting his family, who demonstrated such tremendous solidarity with us. For years, their house was always open to us for anything we needed. Dr. Mignone went with me to the court to petition for the habeas corpus. It was on that day as we were saying goodbye that he told me of the meetings at the Plaza every Thursday at three-thirty, and at the Legislature on Tuesdays and Fridays. That was how I became familiar with the human rights organizations, although I had already heard about them because by 1978 everybody was aware of them due to all the unfortunate things that had been happening. What was going on was known. At that time, who didn't have a notion or wasn't aware of what was happening in the country? Too many barbaric things had already taken place for people not to be aware, including the time a group of Daniel's fellow students collected money to help the Mothers of the Plaza in their fight. We contributed money. And that money was handed over on the Thursday just before Daniel's disappearance—he had collected money at the Atomic Commission.

All the things we were exposed to

And so we started knocking on doors, somewhat unthinkingly because we didn't realize the danger this presented. On that same Sunday morning we went to the Army's First Command, and we asked for an interview with Colonel Gatica. He received us on Monday morning in a very aggressive mood. He wanted to know how was it we knew about him, how we had managed to locate him so quickly. In fact, anybody who wanted to know what was going on in the country knew. Young people at the University knew more or less what contacts could be made at that time because Daniel was not the first to disappear from the Atomic Commission. Other kids had already disappeared.

Later we returned many times to the First Command. A Captain Citrano spoke very highly of Daniel. He went as far as to tell us: "Do you think the military would be so stupid as to get rid of people as valuable as Daniel?" They sent us word through his secretary to arrange for an urgent interview with Harguindeguy. He would tell us where Daniel was. Since we were unable to get the interview, we went to see Castro Madero, and he put us in contact with Ruiz Palacios. Ruiz Palacios was always very courteous to us. In short, they never made themselves unavailable to us...and that raised our hopes that Daniel was alive.

One other person whose help we sought was Dr. Mario Amadeo, who did a lot for Daniel. He made many contacts in the upper reaches of the government since he was a very well connected figure.

Given Mario Amadeo's personality, he was really very supportive. I have several letters from him. In one of them, dated December 11, 1979, he expresses his grief at not being able to help us as much as he would have wished: "My determined and prolonged efforts to locate your son Eduardo Daniel and to return him safe and sound to his home have, until now, proven fruitless. This morning, a person whom I fully trust assured me that there are still hundreds of prisoners whose detention is being kept secret. But I don't have the means to find out—assuming the information is truthful—whether your son is among them because the authorities I consulted have assured me in the most categorical way that there are no clandestine prisoners."

All these contacts made me very hopeful about getting our son back safe and sound. Nevertheless, all of that did not prevent us from keeping up our search and doing the impossible to know through other means what was happening to Daniel. We also saw General Riveros, the

Commander of the Campo de Mayo, who told us that the Army was completely innocent, and that the responsible party was the police. They kill all the kids. They go looking for them and kill them. When we left his office they had us between two rows of armed soldiers with their bayonets aimed at us. And at that moment, I realized how reckless we were for exposing ourselves, because at that point we could also have disappeared. It was quite possible for that to happen in order to stop our inquiries. Really, we have been very lucky.

But nothing could stop us, nothing could paralyze us. Our safety wasn't important. It seemed to us that each thing we did was a message Daniel received from us: that we were fighting for him, for his freedom, for his safety, that we had faith in him, that we knew his way of thinking and acting in life. Wherever we went, nothing could stop us; we went with our heads held high, asking for Daniel.

We also sought the help of human rights organizations. They were like a home to us. We used to go all of the time looking for information and support, collaborating with them, participating in their marches. We always participated with our brothers in their pain.

Dr. Mignone invited me to go to the Plaza, which was where his wife was going, because they are also victims of the repression. And that's how I became part of the circle. In the Plaza I have shared many beautiful moments with the Mothers. We feel bound to each other, very united in our pain. We could share our hopes, our doubts, our fears.... These are dramatic moments in our life, very sad, but when we are together, we feel strong, really we feel strong....

That embrace remained etched in my soul

You ask me how I see Daniel. I see him the way they took him away. The moment he left, never to return, remains etched in me. Another thing that remains deep in my memory is when his appointment at the Commission was rejected. I was very sad and wept, and since he had decided to see a general to review his political background, he hugged me and told me: "Mom, relax, because I haven't compromised myself in any way, and you'll see that everything will come out all right." Even today, I feel that even though eight years have gone by, I can sense him at my back. That embrace remains etched in my soul, his going away as well, his sadness as he was taken away. As you see, he didn't put up any resistance, he gave himself up. Really he was confident that nothing would happen to him.

Daniel's hair was brown, his eyes dark, his skin light. He was tall and of a good weight. He was very fond of sports. He used to play soccer. He played with the Communications Club team and with the University team, too. He was a very affectionate son. When I talk about Daniel, I say that I've not only lost a son, I've lost a companion and a friend. Because he talked about his concerns, you could consult him, seek his advice. From the time he was very young he was always a very good student and a very good companion to his fellow students. At the University, too. He was magnanimous, devoid of any selfishness. Look, among so many beautiful memories, there is one I would like to tell about here. In his fifth grade workbook the teacher wrote: "Daniel: a student who does honor to his school and does credit to the human species."

ENRIQUETA MARONI
mother of
JUAN PATRICIO MARONI and
MARÍA BEATRIZ MARONI DE RINCÓN
and mother-in-law of
CARLOS ALBERTO RINCÓN
abducted April 5, 1977

Our great tragedy started at my home on April 5, 1977. I can't stop associating that date with something my son wrote: "I feel within myself a large capacity to love Our Father. I have faith in Him and in his Spirit's presence, which works, which discerns, which intercedes; the more my faith deepens, the more I feel my need for God grows and I feel the urge to embrace Him and ask for His help. I am asking God at this moment to teach us to pray, I ask Him to help us discern His will and to help us to understand the choices we have made in His name."

I remember again that terrible day, when they raided my house and also my daughter's. They took away my son Juan Patricio, and my daughter María Beatriz, and her husband, Carlos Alberto. Since then, we have been searching for them, and we cannot accept the situation in spite of the time that has gone by; we want the explanation for those deeds, and one based on the truth: those deeds, similar to so many others, during which the armed forces broke into our houses violently, sowing terror and bewilderment. The most terrible part is that starting on that very date, our children served to lengthen the long list of the disappeared.

Absolutely everything that happened from then on is related to that fateful night. In our lives, a "before" and an "after" make their appearance. The fact that such a tragedy did not paralyze us, but on the contrary, stimulated us, is amazing. It gave us strength to start on a path that we had never thought we were going to take. At the outset, we asked, begged, repeated petitions so that we would get some news about our children. Had they been swallowed up by the earth? Afterwards, we confronted the dictatorship directly to demand their return. We were not worried about who was the stronger. Our love for our children made us defy their whole repressive apparatus.

This tragedy took away my most profound religious convictions. I had been brought up in a deeply Catholic household. Now I question my religion and the ecclesiastical hierarchy. I have found proof of how far they are from what the Gospel preaches. The attitude of most of the members of the Catholic Church has made me feel swindled, defrauded. But I am not living in conflict; instead I have been made to see the light in many ways.

What my children were like

My daughter, María Beatriz, and her husband, Carlos Alberto, and my son Juan Patricio as well, wanted to put into practice the Gospel's lessons, not just to preach them.

María Beatriz went to the primary school at San Francisco de Sales, to high school at María Auxiliadora, and she graduated as a Social Worker from the University of Buenos Aires (UBA). She worked at the Health Center in Mataderos.

Juan Patricio went to primary school at San Francisco de Sales and high school at Colegio de los Hermanos Lasalle. After that, he studied Sociology at UBA. He worked as a clerk at Argentine Airlines.

Carlos Alberto Rincón, who married my daughter, María Beatriz, did his primary schooling in a state school, and went to high school at Francisco de Sales and los Hermanos Lasalle, in Flores.

My children and my son-in-law became aware of the marked social injustices that existed and still exist in our country. That is why they participated in Catholic young people's movements and, full of expectation, prepared for Peron's arrival in the country.

I think that they nurtured their Christian and social ideals in our home. My husband and I fully share their ways of thinking and acting.

CHAPTER 4

THE MOTHERS GO TO THE PLAZA

CIRCULATE...

Circulate the policeman said,
and they started to march on that Thursday
like blind hens in a circle
or birds from the South, in Summer whirlwinds.
Circulate, he said
and didn't know he was winding up an endless dance
a circle of love over death
a wedding ring with time
a ring around his own neck.

Pedro Orgambide

A CIRCLE OF LOVE

There is a little ovenbird that takes its place comfortably under one of the mouldings of the "pyramid" in the Plaza de Mayo. I like it. I watch it work. Its persistence is funny. Why do they chase it away if it doesn't really bother anybody? They chase it, and it returns. They chase it, and it returns. But it's useless to drive it away. It has decided to stay. This is the place it has chosen for its progeny. At long last, they are forced to accept its presence. They have opted for giving it a coat of whitewash, so it does not clash, and it remains a permanent part of my geography.

Exactly the same thing has happened with these women. They were not intimidated, not even by weapons, and though they were expelled many times, they returned. Until they too became a permanent part of my geography.

A pyramid with a figure on top which insists on reminding us of a dream of freedom, the little obstinate ovenbird, and the white kerchiefs going round in a circle: all of this brings back the memory of the children I miss.

Yes, each of us Mothers is born again in the circle...every Thursday we are a dispersed army which regroups at three-thirty in the afternoon. One Mother leaves her apron in the kitchen, another her sewing machine, yet another her typewriter. We have to be present at three-thirty in the afternoon, in the afternoon at precisely three-thirty. Not one Mother fails: each time there is one more, then another joins in, and then another.

Our comrades who had to travel to Amsterdam or to Paris could go in peace. They knew that those in the circle would continue and keep backing them up from this far away corner, no matter where they were.

What mysterious hand convoked us? The puzzle of our children's fate, which didn't stop us from going on...the son's photograph on the night table; every Thursday it would point the way—"Today is the circle, Mom;—to the Plaza!"

AND THUS IT STARTED...

Marta Vázquez recounts: "When I first went to join the Mothers, they were still meeting at the entrance of the Church of San Francisco, two blocks from the Plaza. From there we'd start for the Atlántida Publishing House and the *Buenos Aires Herald*, a group of some twenty or thirty women who had signed a letter. And after that, we started to meet at the Plaza. And since we'd hold the meeting at one of the gazebos, where we would always sign a letter, the police began to notice our presence and to say that we could not gather there—because we were already a group of thirty or forty Mothers and so were rather noticeable. They didn't know yet who we were, but something must have made them uneasy, and they started to tell us to circulate, that we couldn't stay there. And that's what gave us the idea of walking all of the time. They'd tell us: "CIRCULATE! CIRCULATE!" And so we started to walk. But at that time we were still walking arm in arm in a formation of five or six across.

One day somebody suggested walking "two by two," and then we started to walk that way, and we realized that this way we were more visible, and we kept on walking like that. We could not stop, because when we tried to stop, they made us keep on walking....

The uniformed police taught us to go around in a circle. During the first years, we went around the flower beds that leads up to the Belgrano Monument. Then we went around the pyramid and the flower beds, until they started to put up fences and we weren't able to get by them. After that, the circle remained for good the way it is today—around the Mayo Pyramid.

ARM IN ARM IN THE PLAZA

My first times in the circle I was very scared, frightened more than scared, and deeply moved. When I was in the Plaza I used to tell myself: "Well, here I am," and I'd even feel safe in spite of the fact that I realized that we were very much under surveillance, watched by young men, by very youthful boys who came wearing jeans, who pretended to be passersby. We were conscious of that, but in spite of everything, we didn't feel afraid in the plaza. What was stressful was getting to the Plaza. It was an incredible feeling. Because during the first days I did not warn my husband that I was going to go—at that moment I don't believe he would have opposed it—but I felt more at ease this way. At the time it was a tremendous effort to get to the Plaza, to the point that sometimes I used to tell myself: "Well, I'm going this Thursday, I don't know what's going to happen there, I am going this Thursday but afterwards I'm not going anymore." And as I moved forward, I kept assuring myself: "I am not going any more. Next Thursday I won't go." But of course, the following Thursday would arrive, and from early in the day, I wouldn't think about anything but going to the Plaza. Actually I could not think about anything else. The degree of physical insecurity didn't allow me to admit to myself, "I am going to the Plaza."

I would only tell myself: "I'll take a walk along Florida Street, and, well, I'll be going along Florida and perhaps I'll get to the Plaza." Other times I'd take a bus that left me a few yards away. Well, that occurred quite a few times. But it did not happen just to me, it happened to many of us.

Once we were in the Plaza, the fact of being arm in arm, or of walking together, compelled us to return. We really wanted the week to go by quickly so we could be together. Something very important that cannot be denied was that since every door, every avenue, every possibility was closed to us, we also came to understand how we soon bored even our relatives and friends, always talking about the same thing and crying. We discovered the reason for the hold the Plaza had on us: we could talk about our concerns without any problem, without fear, and the person by our side listened very, attentively, and would say to us afterwards: "Now let me tell you." I realized very soon that among us women we would tell each other things that we wouldn't even tell our husbands. And so, the first circles at the Plaza had this attraction, but also a disquieting aspect: the realization that we were compelled to go, and also the fear we experienced at being there.

In general, we Mothers made many mistakes— sometimes we acted in a naive and incoherent way. Nearby, with a policeman close at hand, we'd arrange a place to meet by saying: "Let's meet next Thursday in Cabildo to buy a bathing suit." In our innocence we were sure that the police- man was going to really believe that we were going to meet to buy a bathing suit. Or again, we'd agree to meet saying exactly the same thing every time: "Shall we shop for a blue sweater?" And that had a coded meaning, until finally, one of the women said: "It seems to me that every week we're shopping for the same blue sweater, why don't we change its color?" Well, a lot of such silliness. Or we'd agree to meet at the Cabildo itself, and at the other end of the phone line the person would think that it was on Cabildo Street. And that would create great confusion and much discussion afterwards. Then too, some of the Mothers said that it was best to speak with absolute clarity on the phone, because otherwise it was too confusing, and anyway, they already knew that we were meeting and it made no sense to hide it.

At the same time, we felt watched, spied on, and also made fun of. They called us the mad women. At that time we could not dream that the Plaza was going to become a place upon which the whole world would focus its eyes on Thursdays, to such an extent that in many European cities people began to walk in circles of solidarity.

I've met many women who have led the Mothers of the Plaza de Mayo movement practically from its beginnings, and I have admired many of them and followed their example, because of their tenacity above all, and the clarity with which they visualized their objectives: Azucena Villaflor, María Adela de Antokoletz, Hebe de Bonafini, Rosario Cerrutti, Elida de Galletti stand out.

The image of Azucena Villaflor, whom I never knew personally, is the product of the memories the other Mothers brought to me. Sometimes I think that I stood next to her once, sometimes that I didn't. Maybe Azucena was the woman who told me very firmly when I left one of my first walks in the Plaza circle: "Now, when I get off, don't follow me. Get off by yourself at the next stop." By chance, we had taken the same bus. Because of the description I was given of her, I believe this was Azucena: intelligent, decisive, visionary. She was the first one to lead the Mothers' group.

After Azucena's abduction, Hebe Bonafini's image begins to stand out. Her name has become synonymous with our fight all over the world. It seems to me that this woman has a very unusual spirit; her personality put a seal of enormous strength upon the movement, and also the movement put its seal upon Hebe de Bonafini.

One other Mother who showed great initiative and courage was María Adela, whose vehemence and serenity have constituted one of the pillars of the movement.

We had started a new type of struggle which was not any the less valuable because we were ignorant of its real scope. I've always thought that thousands of different types of struggles are possible without resorting to weapons; much of the attraction that the Plaza had was that it was a totally peaceful kind of protest, a really tenacious kind of resistance in the face of the most aberrant violence within our memory—generated by the State itself.

I admire those women whom they called mad, my mad ones, the Plaza de Mayo's mad women. Those Mothers who dared during those years to go out on the street and show their faces, show their tears of anger and desperation. Just across from the very center of power, they managed to blaze one of the most fertile trails in our century. I had never thought they would ever notice me in our city, so removed from the "developed" North: now they know me, but oh horror! Only because they connect me with so much mourning, like somebody lost from civilization's hand. I am a witness to things that shake the whole world's conscience.

THIS SMALL KERCHIEF WAS PAIN'S COMPANION...

Usually everybody asks me, what about the kerchief, when did you start wearing it? I can't remember exactly when, and among us there are different versions of the story. I believe it was when an American named Cyrus Vance came to the Foreign Office with a list of disappeared persons to ask the military authorities for news. And that took place at the Plaza San Martín. We Mothers agreed that we should wear something so that we could recognize each other just in case some of us were detained. At this point we talked about wearing a head-band in the Vietnamese style, or a white handkerchief, which everybody carries in her hand bag. This is what I remember. From then on the kerchief became an irreplaceable item. And this small kerchief became the Plaza de Mayo's symbol every Thursday at three-thirty in the afternoon whether the temperature is comfortable or cold, even when it is below freezing, or during days of torrid heat, in rain or in winds that make our kerchiefs and umbrellas fly away, or even us ourselves!

To our great astonishment, that idea of wearing a white kerchief so that we could easily see and locate each other has taken on gigantic proportions. People know the kerchief in different parts of the world. And other women, in different situations, make the decision to wear it to go out and fight for a cause "like those women over there in that Plaza in Buenos Aires." An Israeli parliamentarian told us that when she was in Beirut participating in marches in favor of Palestinians, a group of Palestinian mothers requested that if any of her trips took her to South America, she should get them the story of those women who "wear a white kerchief and go out in search of their disappeared children, disappeared while defying the dictatorship that governs that country." And that woman gave her promise to go to Buenos Aires to personally find out the story.

TESTIMONIES

for my son, for my daughter,
me, mother in the circle under
the white caress of a kerchief,
a white kerchief with an inscription:
a name, a date.

MARTA VÁZQUEZ
mother of
MARÍA MARTA VÁZQUEZ DE LUGONES
23 years old, abducted with her husband
CÉSAR AMADEO LUGONES
26 years old, on May 14, 1976

María Marta made me go to the shantytown...

Before, I used to think that I understood my daughter, and
now I realize I didn't, in spite of the fact that I took part in
her work. Many times—I don't know whether it was because I saw her working so hard, imbued with that love she
had for others, especially children—I would sometimes
selfishly think that she was risking her health and her life,
because, like her friends, she didn't use a timetable to go to
the shantytown if they needed her. She would stay at night
keeping the children company if their mother was at the
hospital taking care of another little brother. Other times
she and her friends would go to the hospital to help out;
they saved several little ones, because when they realized
that a child was dying, they would pick it up and rush it to
the hospital. They also saved a little one who had fallen
down a well. Listen, they've done incredible things. I used
to see her arriving home overwhelmed because of all that
was happening over there. She lived it, she suffered, it made
her sick.

I remember telling her once—to see if she would react
and change a bit: "But María Marta, this is impossible, I
can't accept your leading this kind of life, worrying so
much about those children when you should come first...."

I know I was hard, harder than my feelings, to see if I
could get her to change a bit.

90

And I'll never forget the look she gave me, her eyes opened wide, as if amazed, while she told me: "Mother, how can you be so insensitive!"

I knew the shantytown in Lower Flores, the area called Belén, where María Marta used to work. There was a very humble shack where two or three priests lived: Father Ricciardelli, Father Vernazza and others who left later. In one of the rooms a little school had been organized to help the children with their homework and to teach them. Since they often lacked teachers, María Marta took me there many times to teach. There was an almost blind nun, Sister Luisa, who lived there—devoted to the children.

And between María Marta, her husband, and the rest of the group that worked in the little school in Belén, they built a child-care facility where Sister Luisa looked after many children so that their mothers could work. The girls would go off and on to help, and I also went once or twice. The little school stayed open until they destroyed it with a bulldozer. But the church, now called the Mother of the People, remains, and Father Ricciardelli is still there.

My family

María Marta is the only one of my children who is a girl. José María (we call him Perucho) and I are the parents of six children. Five boys and María Marta, who is the fourth. I will never forget the day our only girl was born, one of the happiest days of my life. Because after three males, I was expecting another male child, so when the doctor told me "it's a girl," I kept looking at him and could not believe it.

She has been extraordinary from a very young age. Because of José María's occupation—he is a diplomat—we have lived mostly outside the country. We came back to Buenos Aires, where María Marta did her fifth year at the school of Our Lady of Mercy, and there she met Mónica

91

Mignone, with whom she became best friends. They disappeared on the same day. Both of them had chosen to become psychology teachers and went together to Salvador University. They were very close, they worked in the same shantytown. When María Marta started studying at the Mercy School, she began by going to the South with the Sisters to do mission work.

The second time she went South, to Lake Puelo, she met César Lugones, who would become her husband.

They disappeared together, on the very same night. César was doing the same kind of work María Marta did. He was also a very aware kid, and he had worked from a very young age with Sister Luisa in the shantytown. They met at the Association of Christian Youths, preparing for the trip and readying all they had to take. By the second year, or maybe the third, they were already an integral part of that group of kids. It was a mixed group, and they got married the following year. Once married, they kept living the same kind of life because both of them were so very dedicated. They gave so much of themselves.... One of the things I remember is that if one of their companions lost his job, César would ask him to write articles for the magazine for which he used to work so that he could earn something. That's the way both of them were.

When they were kidnapped, María Marta was 23 and César 26 years old, and even worse, César was convalescing from a lung operation. He had been very sick; it was a miracle he had been saved.

He had hardly started to work and was being very careful about himself. I remember that he would sit in the sun at Chacabuco Park, across the street from where they lived. From the first moment of his disappearance, we feared for his health. How innocent we were, thinking that the children were going to return and worrying that perhaps he would not be able to stand the incarceration because of his health.

92

María Marta and César were Catholic militants. I'll just tell you that they were good friends with several priests, and that on the day they got married, five officiated at their marriage rites.

It was a beautiful ceremony. They got married in the Euskalechea College Chapel and the children of the shanty-town went with their guitars and sang all the songs.

María Marta and César always sang in the village with them, because I assure you, both of those kids lived in the village. It was their life; they organized a soccer club and pilgrimages to Luján.

They Left us such a great example of a life well-lived....

Really, confronted with such great pain and sorrow for the loss we have suffered, the fact that these two kids have left us so much, such a great example of a life well-lived, so many lessons, gives me a feeling of happiness inside when I think about it. And that is what gives me strength, it is something that has opened the way for me to do the task we have performed with the Mothers and to go forward. Because if somebody had told me more than ten years ago that I was going to do what I have, I would have never believed myself capable of it.

And you know, another thing I can't forget is the last day I saw my daughter. María Marta disappeared with César on May 14th at dawn. They went after her at her place. But I was living in Mexico at the time with Perucho where he was on a diplomatic mission at the Argentinian Embassy. And we had come back in March, 1976 for our son Carlos' wedding. We stayed until April 8. April 8, 1976 was the last day, but no, exactly on the 7th, because I traveled on the 8th.

On the 14th they disappeared, on May 14th. They went

looking for them at three in the morning. It was an operation that started at eleven in the evening because on the same night they took six of their friends, six or seven, I can't remember now. And they began at eleven in the evening at the house of one of them, at one a.m. at another's, at three a.m. at our children's, who lived in a small apartment across from the park. The only witness was the doorman. They dragged him out violently, they ordered him to open the door and then they screamed at him to leave, but he hid behind the staircase and remained listening and watching. Several of the men stayed downstairs in the entrance hall and some others went up to the apartment. And the doorman says that after a good while they came down and told those who were left on watch downstairs: "We didn't find anything." And others stayed in the cars. The doorman assures us that one of them in the cars wore a uniform. After a while, he saw them brought down and taken out already tied up. The doorman's testimony is the only thing we've been left with; it was he who saw them when he opened the door, who managed to see somebody wearing a uniform outside in the car, in a sort of van, while the rest were all in civilian clothes, fully armed. The apartment was turned upside-down. They took away many things. The key disappeared, no one could go in until forty-eight hours later, and, when this was possible, the apartment door was opened, whereas on the first day her brothers had been unable to get in....

Emilio and Chela's family (Mónica Mignone's parents) talked to my sons and told them about Mónica. My children went to María Marta's place but there was no one there by then, so we don't know if the ransacking that took place in the apartment happened on the same night, or if they came back afterwards to take away the things.

When she lived at home, María Marta was always rebuking me for being obsessed with neatness and cleanliness.

94

She was always telling me: "Mom, how important is all this? What's the sense of it? Why do you worry so much about it? No, it's not important!"...and at that time I was annoyed. And when she was no longer here, after she disappeared—it's something that until even today, after ten years—when I am about to clean a piece of furniture, when I am about to dust, I remember her words and I tell myself: "She was so right! Why do I worry about these material things when there are so many other things that have a much larger meaning." I have learnt from my daughter to be less superficial, that we can use our time in other ways but, regrettably, now when she is no longer here.

My children are all tall, rather lean. She was the opposite, the only one who wasn't tall. She had ash-blond hair, blue eyes, and had a tendency to put on weight. She had wide hips, from Perucho's side. Her nose was like mine, a little bit aquiline. As for her personality, she was cheerful. And being a tremendously responsible girl, she never gave us any trouble, not while in primary or secondary school, nor at the university, never, never anything. She was always very independent, and wherever she was she was a bit of a leader.

She always studied in religious schools. When she was at Our Lady of Belén during her fourth year in high school, the sisters called me, very annoyed. I didn't know what was going on. When María Marta saw an injustice, she didn't keep her mouth shut about it. Small though she was, she had character.

They had had exams and they had included subjects which they hadn't studied the whole year. She didn't remain silent, and she stirred up all the mothers. Everyone complained and the vice-principal called us, furious, and told us: "This cannot be! This girl is too independent!"

Now, looking at her photograph when she was six years old and we were living in Chile, I see that in spite of her age, there was already in her eyes a maturity, a sweetness, there was something that was...ethereal, there was something that was the way she was. And that is the memory that has stayed with us.

Now I look at it, I can look at it. And I feel so much love, something very special. At the beginning, do you know? When I was alone and looked at it, I would start crying like a mad woman. I couldn't stand it, I hugged the photo. True, I would embrace it and cry out and beg.... Now time has taught me that there is another way of living and going forward.

Myself, searching

They disappeared on May 14 at three in the morning, and our sons, Carlos, a lawyer, and Rafael, who is today an agricultural engineer, called us on the phone at dawn on the 15th. Perucho didn't travel for fifteen days because Carlos said to him: "Dad, don't come, we are going to take care of it." And after fifteen days of fruitless attempts, he called asking for one of us to come.

Perucho came and because of the position he held, spent two months trying to get something done at the highest levels; Emilio Mignone went too.

They tried to move everything, everything, everything: the Church, everything they could think of, and...nothing. He came back disheartened, feeling like an old rag. He hadn't managed to get any information. And I tell you that we had good friends in the Army, but there was no one who would tell him this is the way it is, or this isn't the way it is, or anything. After two or three days, these friends blotted themselves off the map, or they promised a lot but did nothing, they started to refuse us...and all of our friends, childhood friends, my family's old friends, families we were friends with, they disappeared, they ignored us, terrible!

That's when, after two months, in October, José María, dismissed from his job, returned to the country. We think this was due to the situation too. In November he stopped working for the diplomatic service and started making inquiries and began to act. During the first year, 1977, and for a long time after, there was always somebody at our place, waiting for her to come back.

Eight or ten months had already gone by since her disappearance. Perucho kept on making inquiries, filing requests, along with Emilio and Chela Mignone.

And one day I stood before my husband (he was used to my always being at home) and I told him: "I'm going with you, I want to go." And so I started to participate in all the inquiries and interviews.

One day Emilio advised us to start going to the interviews by ourselves. And I remember the first time that Chela and I went by ourselves. We went to the Navy Department to see someone on a high level. Like everybody else, he falsely told us that nothing was going on, that they could not give us any information, that they didn't know anything. They thought that we were naive, that we didn't realize what was going on. I continued with this work along with Perucho until May, 1977 more or less. Then Chela let me know that there was a group of Mothers who met in the Plaza de Mayo on Thursdays at three o'clock in the afternoon. So I went to the Mothers of the Plaza de Mayo. Azucena was there, who indisputably had great drive and was very decisive and gave us ideas which we went along with. And so we began to take action together. We'd go to different sites, to Army regiments, to Army Command #1, stand at the entrance door—we'd take turns.

The way my husband came to accept my activity so fully was admirable. He accompanied us a lot, and even when he didn't participate in the circle, most of the time he was at the Plaza. Our husbands were afraid of what could happen to us there.

And I will never forget August, 1977, the first time they detained some of us. It was Marta, Aurora Morea, and myself. This is how it happened: on that day a special security force came to suppress activities in the Plaza. They saw us walking in a circle and they dispersed us very quickly. They would disperse us and we'd separate, get together again, and come back to re-establish the circle around the pyramid. And they'd get very irritated because we weren't going away. We'd leave for a little while and come back. We repeated this trick over and over again for many years: we'd get back together and then get back in a circle. That time, one of the first, when we were coming back, the patrolmen were standing on the Hipólito Yrigoyen side of the Plaza, and we saw that they had one of the Mothers by the side of the patrol vehicle. I remember that I lowered my voice and told Mrs. Morea: "We're not leaving, look, there is a Mother by the patrol wagon, let's see what's going on." And we went around the circle moving towards the patrol vehicle. There were three patrolmen together, and they had her standing next to one of them, and the minute we approached, they got her into the vehicle. Then we walked by them, looked and asked what was going on. They told us very harshly that we didn't have any business there, that we had to leave. I will never forget the expression of the one who was giving the orders, an officer in fatigues. His eyes looked as if they were on fire, and he was shouting at us in an outraged voice: "You don't need to be here! You have to leave!" Mrs. Morea answered by telling him that this was a public Plaza, that it belonged to everybody, that there was no reason for her to leave. And he screamed at her: "Get into the patrol car!" "Very well," she told him. And she looked at me and I told him: "And me too," and so the three of us got into the patrol wagon. And that was the first time they detained somebody at the Plaza.

They only had us for a few hours because my husband was at the Plaza, so Azucena and the other Mothers ran towards him. At that time Ruiz Palacios was the Home Affairs sub-secretary, under Harguindeguy, and he had received us twice. So at the door of the Government Palace, the women found Perucho, who had an audience with Ruiz Palacio. They told him that there were problems, that a woman had been detained. "How? who? and Marta?" "She's one of them," they told him. He became desperate, stirred up the whole Secretariat, got to Ruiz Palacios' office and in two or three hours they gave the order to free us. But while we were at Police Station No. 3, many more detained people arrived, about twenty journalists and people who were going by.

And they kept all the detainees for hours. When my husband got to the Station, the order came from the Ministry to free me, but he said: "No, my wife was detained together with other women. If you don't let all of them leave, she won't leave." And so all three of us who had been arrested were freed, and we waited outside. After two or three hours, everybody started coming out. The men were kept longer.

That's how, without even realizing it, I started to struggle and work with the Mothers, and the group started to develop, to unify, to fight, and without any planning, to confront the dictatorship—which at that time was so horrendous. And for us going to the Plaza every Thursday became a need. It didn't matter how we were feeling because I will tell you, every Thursday, before going to the Plaza, when I woke up and remembered what day it was, my stomach started to ache. This nervous feeling was something so overwhelming that I couldn't find any peace. But it was simply a matter of getting onto the Plaza, and that seemed to calm me down, to fill me with an unknown strength. When I was confronted and was told no, I pushed

99

on, and I fought on two or three occasions. How I did it, I don't know.

We knew that they were listening on our phone lines, that we were being watched all of the time, but also that what we were doing was something that was not against the law, that it was human, that is was legal, that we didn't have anything to hide. And so we kept on marching ahead, talking to each other on the phone. When we wanted to say that we had a meeting, we'd say: "We're going to play canasta." "We're going to sew." Others would say, "We're going to do some embroidering." And so it went on like this for a long time, until the Association of Mothers of the Plaza de Mayo was formed. Just the same, we kept on meeting in our houses until we had our first house on Uruguay Street. Then all the meetings took place there. The group had grown a lot.

The Mothers' group was incredible. When somebody new arrived, nobody—ever—would ask her who she was, or where she came from. Sometimes we had doubts about some people coming for the first time, but usually we recognized when they were working for the security services. Then we acted in such a way that they wouldn't come back—they felt exposed. And afterwards, since it was a group in which we leaned on each other, the strength that one of us lacked on a certain day, another had for that occasion. The other had words of consolation, for pushing us to keep on going, words of valor, of courage, and so we kept on. And I believe that all these small brushes that we had with the police and the security forces, instead of intimidating us, gave us more courage, mobilized us even more.

The forces of repression caused the disappearance of Azucena and the French nuns—for Sister Alicia also walked with us. They thought that we were going to stop gathering at the Plaza, but it didn't happen, we didn't get scared. I will never forget it, it was something so incredible. I met

Esther Careaga, who marched with us, on Avenida de Mayo, across from the *La Prensa* newspaper office, and I asked her: "What are you doing here?" Her disappeared daughter had been freed. "Don't come any longer, you'll put yourself in danger." And her answer: "But this is something stronger than me. Even if it is only from this spot, I have to see you." She stayed at the edge of the Plaza border...she told us that she couldn't stop coming.

I believe that Azucena's disappearance made us stronger. I will never forget her last words to us. She disappeared when we were preparing the Open Letter with the names of eight hundred disappeared which came out on December 10, 1977 in the *La Prensa* daily. I remember we were checking the lists at the house of one of the Mothers, and she lifted her head, looked at us and said: "If something happens to me, you keep on, don't forget that." We spread her message. And we made good on it.

Preaching any ideology was something we did not allow. The only thing that moved us, always, has been the search for our children. All the actions we have undertaken were directed towards that goal. Even if during this period we failed to obtain the results we were seeking—our children's reappearance, alive—I believe we have obtained quite a bit. We have managed to spread the knowledge of the horror we have been living under for so many years, the massacre that's taken place, this genocide. We have let our country and the whole world know what has happened here. And I think this is quite a bit.

I can tell you that I began this fight and kept it up because of the support I got from my family because I don't know if I would have been able to do it alone. My husband always backed me up, and so did my sons. The way they pushed me to continue was really incredible. They thought that our way of doing things, disorganized, you might say, was the factor that made it hard to wipe us out, because if they had wanted to they could have done it. It is possible that they didn't attach importance to us, that they didn't believe we were going to achieve what we achieved.

Many times I wanted to stop. I felt embittered, tired: "You have to go on, you have to go there," and if we had to travel, with all the sacrifice of leaving the family behind, I would go because my family pushed me to go. And I believe that the same thing happened to many of the Mothers. My sons adored their sister.

Understanding what has happened cost us very dearly, and I would say that until a very short time ago, we were still waiting for our children. Because of what they have taught us, I now think that the model of their lives, their sacrifice, hasn't been in vain. Because all the children, not just mine, were alike. I'd talk to another of the Mothers and her son seemed to be my son. They have taken away the best of our young people, and that cannot be forgotten, that has to be remembered always. This marvelous sacrifice of youth has to remain forever in our memories. To achieve this, above all so that we learn that this can never be repeated, so that our young people enjoy the right to live in peace and in freedom, we Mothers keep on fighting and will always fight.

But I don't want to close my testimony without telling about the last image I have of my daughter. On May 7, 1976, María Marta and César came to say goodbye at my parents' house because they were unable to go to Ezeiza Airport on the following day. And when they were already in the elevator, I told them: "Children, be careful, don't work so hard, don't be so open...." And she, with her angelical smile, looked at me from the back of the elevator and answered: "But Mom! What are you thinking of! Why do you worry so much?" And she told me this with a great smile. That was the last thing that María Marta said to me. And I watched her slowly descend in the elevator shaft. And thus she disappeared from our lives, as if the earth had swallowed her up.

ANGELICA P. SOSA DE MIGNONE
mother of
MÓNICA MARÍA CALANDERIA MIGNONE
abducted on May 14, 1976 at 24 years of age

My daughter was born in Luján. There she went to primary school. In 1962, the whole family left for the United States because of my husband Emilio's job, and there we lived for five years. Mónica finished grammar school there and began high school. When back in Buenos Aires, she graduated from the Sisters of Mercy High School in the Belgrano neighborhood. That was in 1968. Then she studied psychopedagogy at the University of Salvador. When she was abducted from our home, she was working as a teaching assistant at the University of Luján, and was training at Piñero Hospital.

In addition, she had some patients at home. Mónica lived with us and her brothers in an apartment downtown on Santa Fe St. They took her from there, from our own home, with all of us present. An armed forces team came on May 14, 1976 at five o'clock in the morning.

Since then we haven't heard anything about her. The armed forces as well as the Argentinian government have refused to give us any information. As regards the petitions for habeas corpus which we presented to the Executive Power—the civilian and military authorities deny the detention. However, there is proof that Mónica was detained by agents of the armed forces and the security forces.

I remember Mónica's many qualities and virtues, above all, her generosity. She gave help to her next of kin, her brother, without measure or calculation. She was a very good student, cheerful and hard working and to us she was a loving daughter. And she was also an exemplary friend.

Truly, Mónica lived for everybody. She undertook missionary work with all her heart. But her major giving of

103

herself was at the Bajo Flores shantytown. She didn't keep count of the hours, the days or the nights. She simply loved the villagers, she understood them, she felt them to be her equals. And she devoted herself to the children because she loved justice above any personal interest.

She gave of herself to her brothers, the poor, the distressed, the sick. She fought with a passion for all of them. That's why I say that they took her away, because she was better than us. The only thing that gives me some consolation is to repeat the Gospel's phrase: "Happy be they who are hungry and thirst for justice, for they shall be satisfied."

I would like you to include this piece Mónica wrote, which has also been included in the book *From the Silence*.

The Neighborhood of "Belén" in the temporary "villa" of Bajo Flores (1974)

When it is cold, it's even colder here. And when it's hot, it's hotter here than in other places in Buenos Aires.

But on Saturday afternoons, there are people in the street. The children play and you can hear music coming from everywhere.

I walk along Riestra Street and a thousand faces greet me from their houses, from the water taps and from the stores. The children see me from afar. They have incredible eyesight. They come running and throw themselves on my neck and give me a kiss.

Only seldom do we see a car on the villa streets. The children, barefooted, play in the mud or throw things in the ditch that gives the neighborhood a fetid smell.

The vacant lot, which is used as soccer field, is always occupied on Saturdays. Whether it rains or not, the team comes, and so do their fans, though sometimes I fail them.

Belén changes with the weather. We feel the sadness on cloudy or rainy days because you can't go out. People only go out because they need to go to work or because they need to buy something. The mud swallows your feet when you step in it, but it seems to have more respect for those from Belén than for the outsiders. The villagers wear sandals or old shoes. On cloudy days the villa has a special color—of loneliness, of marginality. You see people cleaning water out of their houses. Huge leaks in their roofs let water drain inside and it has to be caught in pots, pitchers or buckets.

In the villa you know your neighbor, you know who he is. The children stay with this or that neighbor. When a person is sick, someone will always come by to give advice or medicine. The grocers sell on credit. They know that there are people who are very exploited and who cannot pay.

The cops often appear. One day I got scared. That day the cops passed through Belén, but they only passed through. I asked where they were going. Oscar explained to me that they were going to the grocer's to wheedle merchandise out of him. They tell me it's always been this way. If the grocer refuses them, they accuse him of being a numbers man.

So many things like that happen there. But the villager is destined to be silent. The law doesn't protect him. It only protects the rich.

JOSEFINA GANDOLFI DE SALGADO
mother of
JOSÉ MARÍA SALGADO
abducted when 22 years old, March 12, 1977 and
murdered on June 2, 1977

We had trouble recognizing him

Two months after the news of our son's death, we had lost
hope of recovering his corpse, when we got an appointment at the First Command. My husband went there
immediately and was given an authorization to remove the
body from the Justice Department Morgue.

On June 3, the Armed Forces Command, using every
means of communication, put out a story concerning his
death in a confrontation with security forces near 400
Canalejas Street. According to them, the car in which he
was fleeing along with two other "subversives" was
intercepted.

It was then that my sad pilgrimage started to all the
places where we might claim his body. I myself went to the
Army posts in Palermo, police stations, the Government
House, and the Department of the Interior. From there
they sent me to an office on Moreno Street, where there
was an impressive line of people coming to protest
disappearances. I was asking for my dead.

I don't want to remember the humiliations I was
subjected to, and which, honestly, I don't know how I was
able to endure. They were another burden added to the
three months of anxiety caused by the disappearance on
March 12, 1977.

At the Command Post, they didn't even receive me. You
were forbidden to cross the street and get near the guard.
At the Department of the Interior they asked me ironically
if I was looking for a terrorist's body.

106

Finally, with the Command's authorization, we went to the Morgue. There we were read document #1331, and then they brought us the coffin. It was July 27.

I told them I wanted to identify him, my husband didn't have the strength to look at him. Just my eighteen-year-old daughter and I wanted to see him.

I never thought there were people in this world so depraved that they could reduce a human being to the state in which they left my son. Nor could I explain to myself how two desperate women could continue to stand on their feet while looking at those poor remains—covered with newspapers. He had been sadistically destroyed alive. It was hard to recognize him. I think it was his light brown hair, abundant and soft, that told us it was our dear boy. Both eyes were missing, and his mouth was open in a terrible grimace of pain, showing his destroyed teeth, which had no resemblance at all to his perfectly white ones, visible only a short time ago when my son laughed in his frank and easy way. Consumed, he looked as if it was not two months but years of deprivation that had gone by in order to turn this twenty-two year old boy into the suffering body we saw before us. Upon looking at him, without wanting to, I remembered the outwardly compassionate words of a neighbor who believed the news of the spurious confrontation and who had said to me: "Don't you see, Josefina, you were suffering desperately, thinking that your son had been abducted, and he was living in hiding without worrying about the pain he was causing you."

How they lied to almost the whole country! How easy it was to make us look crazy, those of us who made a fuss so that they would give us back our loved ones!

Nothing was left of our healthy, happy, intelligent son who, a few months before, had gotten married and was waiting impatiently for his first child.

From the morgue we went directly to Chacarita Cemetery, where we wanted to cremate him and then bring

107

his ashes home. My husband and my daughter got into our car, but I wanted to go with him, and I sat next to the coffin.

In spite of the sad state in which we started our trip, from the moment we left, how many good moments of our son's life came into my mind, this son who had filled us with happiness and satisfaction from the moment he came to this world, twenty-two years earlier, on January 17, 1955.

He was our third child, our third boy.

When he was five he became a boy scout, just like his brothers. He was the wolf-scout Pepe, always cheerful, always ready for any task he was assigned. The priest, Father Aníbal Coerezza, would tell me that he was too good. "He is going to be a priest," he insisted.

He radiated friendliness

At the Institute Jesús in the Orchard of the Olives, where he went to primary and secondary school like his brothers, I only heard words of praise, not only from his teachers, but also from the families of his fellow students. When he finished his last year, he received the valedictorian's medal.

Who could have guessed that his life, so rich in personal experiences, was going to be so short and that it would end so tragically?

He got married very young, when he was twenty-one years old, to a fellow student in the College of Engineering, and it was a pleasure to see them so happy, struggling to be able to study and work. Happy as two children, they were expecting their first child. All that energy, that vigor, that strength was in that small box I had traveling now beside me.

He was a very nice kid, he radiated friendliness. He was twenty-two years old and his face was always happy, with dark eyes, brown hair; he was five feet and seven inches tall, slender but strong. He had done rowing and enjoyed sports.

The horror began on Saturday, March 12, when they abducted him around 4:30 p.m. in Lanús near his house.

All of our pride and our happiness consisted of seeing our children grow. It burst when the phone rang and Pepe's voice said: "I am being detained at Federal headquarters."

In spite of the fact that we knew that the children of some acquaintances had disappeared—neighborhood friends—so far did we believe ourselves from the possibility that he could be detained that I asked him to please refrain from making such a tasteless joke.

To corroborate that he had been detained, I listened to a clearly authoritarian voice insist that it wasn't any joke and that my son had been detained and accused of being a subversive. It will soon be ten years since that moment. But for a long time I remained so broken-up that when I answered the phone, I believed that I was hearing that voice again. I believe that my life stopped at that moment, and I don't know if it was sadism or some dirty trick from the barracks, but the speaker gave the phone back to my son who, now with a different voice, said to me: "Mother, please, help me!" And he added before he was cut off: "If you knew what shape I am in!"

Forgive us, my son, we were unable to help you. We did all but the impossible to try to find your whereabouts from the moment you called us, and that's when our Calvary began.

My husband, a lawyer, took the legal part in his hands: the search. I wore down every sidewalk and rang every door bell wherever I suspected there was somebody who could give me a hand to find out where he was.

The first one we consulted was General Viola, who was a colleague of my brother-in-law, General Salgado. My father-in-law was sure, since they were old friends, that he would find out where he was. He was wrong. Viola never answered his request.

I took the responsibility of talking to priests and bishops, and I suffered the worst letdowns in my life. I have great faith in God, which I instilled in my children (three boys and two girls), and I brought them up in the bosom of the Catholic Church.

Both my husband and I devoted ourselves to its service. I did this with my music, playing the organ over many years.

I should have recorded the conversation I had with Monsenior Aguirre, Bishop of the diocese of San Isidro, to which we belonged. I left the Archbishopric sick. I believe that at the peak of the Inquisition you could not have found a harder and more insensitive inquisitor. I only wish God may have mercy on him.

We took refuge in a church that was far away, in Acassuso, because there we found a priest's warm friend-ship and support. He had known our children since they were young, and he wept with us in our anguished sorrow. This was Father Agustín.

Thus we arrived, in this whirlwind of remembrances, at the Administration of Cemeteries, to seek the authorization for the cremation. We were met with surprising news. Since his death was recorded as having happened during a con-frontation, we would need the permission of the First Command, so they advised us to bury him in a plot or in a niche.

We went back with our dear charge to the funeral parlor to have him put in another coffin. When they did this, I asked them to let me place a rosary in his hands. Only then did I realize the atrocious condition of his hands and arms, covered with circular brownish spots which I later learnt were the burn scars left by electric shock. His hands were almost cut off at the wrist, because the identification encircling them reached the bone. I suppose that during his entire imprisonment his hands were tied.

I wanted to look at the rest of his body, but they didn't let me.

Back in the car on our way to Chacarita but now weighed down by the horrendous vision of José María's condition, I thought I was going mad.

I remembered then how depressed I was on March 19, Saint Joseph's day. It was just a week after he had been detained, and we were living in uncertainty about his pregnant wife's situation.

That evening there was a knock at the door, and I could not believe it: it was her. A relative brought her home. She was safe.

How strong my daughter-in-law was! It is true that she went through moments of fully justifiable despondency, but her serenity inspired us, and gave us strength to keep on living.

We were preparing the layette for the baby with so much hope and happiness that nobody could have guessed that each of us when out of sight of the others carried such a heavy sorrow.

We were told that their house had been ransacked. We went there to find a scene of desolation. They had looted it. No furniture was left or kitchen utensils or eating equipment, or clothes, or domestic necessities, or the car, nothing.

Do you remember, Pepe, the Sunday before your abduction, when you were leaving our house late in the evening, your car filled to the top with the things that we had been preparing for your small house, the curtains for all the windows which we had sewn, the bed clothes?

The baby's room was a surprise. You didn't want to tell us what color the paper would be. After the ransacking, we saw it: they had torn it all off, and the strips were piled on the floor. Later we supposed that when you had finished papering the walls, you felt very tired and went out for a walk. You never came back.

In such a climate, the day of birth was getting near.

So, June 3 arrived and with it the news of my son's death during a confrontation. Using the most refined hypocrisy, they wanted to hide behind a calumny the horror of the abduction, the torture, the sacking, and death.

On June 20, Flag Day, the baby was born—a little boy. We were happy because we had a piece of our son, something that he had left us. It seems as if he knew that he had to get married, that his life would be short. I don't know what to say. He wanted to leave us that gift.

And we felt an immense sorrow when we remembered that a few days before the abduction he had told me: "Ah, Mom, why do babies have to take such a long time getting here? I can't wait to see him!" And he told me this a week before his abduction. He never saw his son.

And in addition to the pain and the impotence we felt in wanting to shout: It's a Lie! There was the baseness of the threats! Anonymous voices on the phone announced to us that the whole family would die. That was another part of their plan: to terrorize us.

Our decision to stay

As a precaution my daughter-in-law left. To keep living in our house meant a very great risk. They wanted all of us to leave. The threats, the well-intentioned advice from some friends and relatives, they were all part of a sinister plan.

My husband and I listened daily to these "siren songs," and he was about to give in. I was not deceived. My attitude was firm. The decision to stay was very difficult, but we took it. This meant that the next step of their plan failed. Our desertion would have meant a tacit acceptance of our son's culpability, and we rejected this outright.

So we arrived at your last dwelling place. Six people formed the cortege accompanying you. Six trembling hands were sufficient to carry that coffin, which weighed so little. Without tears, without complaints. The pain was too great. In a few days, it will be ten years since that moment. Ten years during which so many things have happened.

I fell into a depression. We watched friends, relatives, neighbors, and work companions distancing themselves from us. We also saw people arrive with handshakes and words of consolation from whom we would never have imagined such gestures could come.

One day in desperation I wrote Arbishop De Nevares, telling him about our experience.

He gave me back my lost peace and hope. He advised me to look around me for those who were in greater need of consolation. I did. I joined the Mothers of the Plaza de Mayo.

I met a neighborhood couple whom I had never seen before. I approached them because I found out that their only child had been taken. The husband was disabled. I wanted to offer them a word of consolation, and in a short time I realized that Don Arturo, even without his legs and brokenhearted, was going to be my pillar, the one who would support me.

I keep on with the struggle as I had on the first day after my son's abduction. More tired, older: now I am alone. A few months ago, my husband fell sick with a terrible illness that consumed him cruelly until it killed him. He fell mortally wounded on the day that he realized all the weapons the law had placed in his lawyer's hands were of no help to recover his son.

I found out that José María was held in detention clandestinely at ESMA (the Argentinian Navy School). That he was tortured there "by courageous Navy boys," "the virile and bold-hearted ones,"—especially when it meant mistreating defenseless women and keeping the babies of the mothers in shackles who gave birth there. I found out that from there they took him to the internal security branch of the Federal Police, where an illustrious police chief murdered him. Too bad his name isn't known, so that history can remember him and give him the honors due him!

I was a witness to the parody of a trial, where there wasn't enough proof to condemn these perpetrators of genocide.

Never mind. I will keep on fighting in spite of all the "statutes of limitations," because there cannot be a *punto final*, a statute of limitations, on a mother who wants to know the truth about the death of her twenty-two year old son. I WANT JUSTICE.

CHAPTER 5

THE STRUGGLE AND THE DICTATORSHIP

A Mother

Everybody in the neighborhood knows what happened.
But we just help her cross the street
and say "good morning."
Later in the day, someone comes saying he saw her
at the Plaza, or he saw her at the capitol, but
we remain silent. We feel fear and compassion
when we see her come home, with the night
in her eyes, embraced by the past,
and the power of what is to come.

Gustavo Zappa

WHAT ELSE IS THERE TO DO, WHAT ELSE IS THERE TO TRY? WE WERE BORN AGAIN....

To be born again means to find or to discover the true meaning of existence.

It means to find what is legitimate and what is false, superfluous, fatuous.

To become conscious that if we are to survive, we must manufacture, work, produce something for others, for those who come after us.

To repudiate, to utterly condemn a past of injustices and abominations, to cry out for ourselves, and to protect the right to life for the generations that are to come.

It means to become more receptive to feelings and to pledge ourselves to a specific struggle.

Life is totally different now. We begin by recycling and reevaluating everything that surrounds us. Even the most subtle thing acquires a new form. As for myself, in recollecting my previous life, I separate out everything which is not useful either to me or to our search. I live much more among symbols, too, and gratifying recollections. On the other hand, my feeling of guilt grows stronger, and I am tormented by memories of mistreating my daughter, or pressuring her, just as my mother had done to me, to get her to obey my rules. This is a theme that we would talk more about among the Mothers in due time, as well the feelings of guilt for not having moved more quickly and more urgently because of that damned paralysis fear produces at first. And the lack of immediate answers. In this way our lives were changed.

There are no tabu subjects. Life changes you because there is no recess. Minute by minute you squeeze your brain, dig in it and search for what more you can do, what else you can figure out...to find your children.

PUEBLA, JANUARY 1979

In her testimony, Marta Vázquez says: "In one of the many trips we took to try to reach the highest authorities, five of us Mothers went to Puebla in January, 1979. In Puebla CELAM was meeting and the Pope's visit to Mexico made us think that we could contact him. We were in Puebla for several days and Nora and I went back to Mexico City to conduct some business. One morning, we left our lodgings to go to the Curia, and we found ourselves on a big avenue where there were lots of people.

"They told us that the Pope was going to come by. We looked at each other and made an instant decision. We ran to a bookstore, bought some paper and an envelope and wrote a short note to His Holiness, John Paul II, and we found a spot there with all the people. Seeing that time was passing and that the Pope was not making an appearance, we inquired and were told that he was at a college some fifteen blocks away. We then took a taxi and left for that spot. We ended up on a road where we were told he was going to pass by. Both of us stood there, each of us with a letter in her hand. One or the other of us was going to get near him. My assignment was to walk towards the entrance, and as I was walking, I saw a large car full of people. I realized that it was the Pope's car, and I began to run. I ran at an incredible speed, as if I were mad, so fast that from the vehicle several bishops saw me coming and started to encourage me by making signs to hurry up.

"When I got there, the bishops pointed behind me. I kept on running, and what happened? At that moment, the Pope had gotten out of the open vehicle and gotten into a closed one. I arrived and began to comprehend what was going on while I kept on running. Just as I arrived at the car it started off and I remained standing there almost crying, letter in hand. Nora had stayed at the entrance path, which connects with the highway. We were lucky because the security guard, which was on motorcycles, had lost the Pope, and the Pope's car was by itself. Nora was waiting for him with her letter. As she saw him arriving, the people surrounding her assisted her, helped her, pushed her and Nora put the letter into the Pope's hand. In the letter, we asked him in the name of all the Argentinian Mothers of the disappeared to intervene and to do everything he could. Because of our despair, it was an anguished, simple petition, a short letter. We remained where we were. When we got back together, we embraced and cried, surrounded by people who didn't know who we were, but who cried with us. That's the way we accomplished what we did. I don't know what, but something was guiding us—for sure. In this same way we have done many things— I would say most of them—always trying to do whatever would get our children back."

WE ARE VISITED BY AN ISRAELI REPRESENTATIVE

On one occasion, with the arrival of Mr. Navon from the State of Israel, a group of us—Jewish mothers and fathers— went to demonstrate at the entrance of the Coliseo Theatre, where a demonstration had been organized. We were carrying signs asking for our children and soliciting his help.

We were wearing the kerchiefs on our heads so that we wouldn't be mistaken. We practically threw ourselves on the car. Some of the mothers stood in front of it to prevent it from moving. But on orders from the Ambassador, we were given a good thrashing under the eyes of the tranquil and complacent Federal Police, who didn't stir. Rabbi Marshall Meyer's son and I received a good beating. Indoors, a few minutes later the visitor spoke, very worried about the incident and he invited us to come in to talk. But the Israeli Ambassador and his guards barred our entry, so that everything was reduced to an exchange of insults between our group and the Embassy guards. As you can see, we were not viewed sympathetically by those people.

We weren't very lucky with them. I regretfully recall that during the dictatorship's most miserable moments, some representatives of the Jewish community actually traveled to the United States to help clean up Videla's image.

THE THEORY OF THE TWO DEVILS

One day during a demonstration, while the Plaza was brimming with people, I left the circle looking for a cafe. I had spent the night in the plaza and was hungry.

There were two well-marked worlds: the Plaza—one of contained fury, protest, impotence in the face of the genocide, and screaming—screaming for life. Away from the Plaza—the world of business, of executives, of those who have real power and for whom the military were the armed instrument.

I crossed the street and took off my kerchief and an enormous shawl. I saw many people standing and observing the Plaza like a curiosity. I passed by two middle-aged men, both a bit grey and exquisitely dressed; one of them made a nervous gesture while looking at his watch, practically pulling the sleeve out of the other's jacket. This other individual was saying in a loud voice: "Wait a minute, those are the Mothers, I want to see what their mugs are like." So I touched his arm and I told him in a quiet voice: "If you want to see the Mothers' mugs, take a good look at my face." And then, how can I explain it? They became stock still and dumbfounded. Nevertheless, the one who wanted to see our "mugs" asked me: Señora, what happened to you? But then it's true? And I quickly said: "I am one of them. They took away my daughter." And he said in a hurry: "What happened? Where?" I explained my case in a few words. At that time, for reasons of security we were very careful about becoming separated from the group and talking to strangers, so that I got away quickly. I only remember that he remained very quiet, deep in thought. And going back to my group, I thought, furious: "Now that guy is going to excuse himself by using the famous two devils' theory."

The first time I heard about this theory was from Dr. Emilio Mignone. His interpretations perplexed me greatly but at the same time made clear to me a situation that has always been much argued over.

"We call the two devils' theory the interpretation which views the situation of violence in Argentina starting in the decade of the '70s as due to two equally diabolical and symmetrical causes: on the one side, subversive activity, and on the other, terrorism applied by government's armed forces. According to this concept, both sectors would be similarly responsible, and this is why they must be condemned by society and judged by the courts of justice.

"This position has been maintained again and again by Dr. Alfonsín and is accepted, in general, by people who condemn the illegal repression exercised by the armed forces, but who consider it to be a consequence of things that took place earlier.

"Those of us who do not adhere to this theory consider that there are quantitative and qualitative differences between the armed actions carried out by civilians for political reasons and the State's terrorist actions. Therefore, the two devils' theory is not correct.

"In the first place, the delinquent acts committed by civilians are subject to the norms of the penal code and to judicial power. Those affected and the State have the possibility of recourse to that power. They are protected, besides, both by security and police forces.

"In contrast, the victims of State terrorism don't have any protection. Moreover, it is inadmissible for the State, created to protect its inhabitants, to become a terrorist and criminal force. To this point, its responsibility becomes greater, and cannot be compared to the actions of civilians.

"In the case of Argentina, the State could have applied the existing penal laws. It didn't do this and preferred to transform itself into a delinquent and a terrorist. For that purpose it utilized the whole state structure, including the judicial power which was created for the defense of its inhabitants.

"Consequently, it is not a question of two devils but simply of one. The system of disappearances utilized, as Julio Cortázar said, is diabolical."

ARE THEY DEAD? WHY? HOW? WHERE?

We mothers have never been given an appointment to inform us officially of what became of our children.

They simply expected us to presume that as the logical consequence of such a prolonged absence they had died. We Mothers saw very many young people being wrenched from their homes, while other parents didn't even see this take place because their children were "sucked up" off the street, or taken upon leaving a meeting or from their work places. No civilized society accepts giving a human being up for dead without any explanation for his failure to return—as if he had vanished into thin air.

121

Periodically, they tossed us the news that all the disappeared were dead. They did it in a surreptitious way, taking advantage of circumstances foreign to the issue. In April, 1980, the Mothers felt obliged to answer a letter from Mr. Balbín, who in reference to the disappeared had twice stated: "Everybody knows that they are dead," but without explaining how he had learnt this.

In our letter of response we demanded the information that Balbín seemed to be manipulating and we reacted to a paragraph which apparently spoke in the name of all the members of the Radical Party: "We'd rather have mothers crying over their dead than begging for an answer." Our response was: "...we Mothers are not begging for an answer, we are demanding it in the name of justice at its most basic, because it is our right."

THE MOTHERS ON THE WAR

*"The Malvinas belong to Argentina,
and so do the disappeared."*

A few days after Galtieri's government initiated its activities concerning the Malvinas (Falklands) war, the Mothers of the Plaza de Mayo established their position of opposition in an open letter:

> The Mothers of the Plaza de Mayo, who know deep pain because of the absence of our "detained-disappeared" children, express our grief for the loss of young lives in the present armed conflict. We exhort the officials responsible in both governments to search immediately for a peaceful solution which will prevent new bloodshed.
> MOTHERS OF THE PLAZA DE MAYO

The series of communications sent by the Mothers to the media reiterate this position, based on the UN's resolution No. 512 which establishes three points: the cessation of hostilities, the Argentinian withdrawal from the islands, and the start of negotiations.

The issue of whether it was prudent to continue our Thursday circles was raised during these difficult moments. Though we were advised to temporarily suspend them because of the fear of violent reactions and of our being accused of being unpatriotic, attendance at the Plaza continued, although it was somewhat reduced. As a matter of fact, there were provocations and even physical assaults. On April 29, while some of the Mothers were holding banners that read: "The Malvinas are Argentinian and so are the disappeared," a group of individuals tried to halt the circle by shouting, "Long live Argentina" while throwing fliers that read, "The friend of our country's enemy is our enemy." This episode reinforced our will to continue the circles.

Also during those days, García Márquez, the Colombian writer, put forward his opinion on the Malvinas while referring to the Mothers:

BOGOTA, 11 (ANSA).—The Colombian writer, Gabriel García Márquez, says in his column today that "the Malvinas Islands belong to Argentina," and he points out that Great Britain's sending of its war fleet "has done no more than repair humiliation with ridicule," but he also strongly criticizes the Argentinian government.

"Whatever might be the outcome of this naphthaline war, next Thursday morning General Galtieri won't be able to avoid the demonstration in the Plaza de Mayo of the ever-present Mothers, whose fifth anniversary is coming in a few days...," states García Márquez.

He also expresses the idea that "the status of the disappeared is perhaps the most painful and serious of Argentinian realities."

He adds, "We agree: the Malvinas belong to Argentina. In this sense, General Galtieri has done no more than to put things in their place. But he has done it in a legitimate act with a twisted end. The British Crown, on the other hand, by sending a fleet of forty war ships with a prince on board, has done no more than to try to repair humiliation with ridicule."

A HELPING HAND FROM HOLLAND

During one of their European tours trying to get solidarity and support for the Mothers, María Adela and René arrived in Amsterdam. They met with a group of Dutch women to whom they told our heartbreaking story. These ladies, among whom Mrs. Liesbeth den Uyl van Vessem stood out, were about to start a human rights campaign to investigate the situation in the Soviet Union, from which they received many complaints. After meeting these Argentinian women, they decided to direct their efforts towards our movement.

The organization formed by these twenty-five women, "SAAM," decided to finance the acquisition of a house in Buenos Aires to function as the Mother's Center, so that "they might have a place where they can be together and talk about their concerns."

Mrs. Liesbeth herself described the impression the drama of the disappearances in Argentina made upon her. It made her abandon her Soviet project to give herself entirely to helping the Mothers.

For us it meant the achievement of a longed-for place of our own where all our children could also be present by means of photographs and posters, and where we could feel quite sheltered. The Mothers' feverish activity with the numerous national and international organizations which were backing us started here. The house also served as a place to organize the Mothers' help and support for the families of the disappeared who lacked resources. Many of the Mothers who came from the provinces found warmth of companionship there and a place of their own.

In May 1982, we dedicated the house. Mrs. Liesbeth had come specifically to Buenos Aires for the occasion, so we decided to organize a circle with more impact, one lasting several hours. Although Mrs. Liesbeth was warned not to come to the Plaza—her Consulate was of the opinion that she was running a risk because the police might attempt to intervene in the demonstration—she decided to accompany us. One of the objectives of her group was "to be with the Mothers, not just help them financially, but to be with them physically." Her attitude when she was faced with the intimidating presence of the police increased our fervor, so that we had a very large and vibrant crowd in the Plaza. We Mothers are equally thankful to the innumerable organizations and groups from different parts of the world without whose help it would have been very difficult to keep up our protest at an international level.

ONE CIRCLE THAT MULTIPLIED INTO MARCHES

Our feet walk by themselves, we can no longer stop them. The urgent need to go beyond the geographical space of the Plaza overcomes us. Perhaps inspired by the marches that the Europeans made in order to side with us, we want to organize other walks, move in other city environments.

We received pictures in which we discovered the faces of very important figures who have gotten out on the streets to ask for our children, like a mirror that projected our image. And we all know that mirrors multiply images ad infinitum.

125

This was the beginning of our own organized marches: from the time they were announced, until they took place, to the moment they ended, they were for us a highly charged event that demanded large amounts of energy. What great expectations they brought us! And what a feeling of having reached a goal!

MARCHES OF RESISTANCE: THE CIRCLE SEES THE DAWN

We Mothers went back to the street again, but this time for many hours. Desperate because of our lack of answers and because of our urgent need to communicate with the people, what else could we do? Press releases, open letters, standing in front of barracks, of government offices.... We needed to do something different. At the end of 1981, thanks to the creativity of some of the mothers, we decided to organize a circle just like the one we did every Thursday at the Plaza, at the same Plaza, but for a longer time. It would be a circle which would be called a March of Resistance and it would last for twenty-four hours.

Would they allow us to occupy the Plaza for so many hours? And how could we keep a circle going for so long without interruptions, without altering its rhythm? Would we have the strength, would our legs hold out? What if an old woman felt sick or exhausted? Could we stand on our feet awake so many hours? One of the Mothers offered, "If we drink *mate* and coffee continually, we won't fall asleep." But another asked: "And how are we going to retain so much liquid?" At that moment we saw it as an adventure far beyond our strength; besides, what kind of repercussions would it have?

Finally, on December 11, 1981, starting at three-thirty in the afternoon, the Mothers, together with some thousand other people, started their First March of Resistance at the

Plaza de Mayo, continuously going around the pyramid. On that day, the thirty-third anniversary of the Universal Declaration of Human Rights was commemorated.

The march was completely nonviolent, but nevertheless the police were there at the Plaza all night long (protecting us?) and surrounded it to prevent people from joining in. They even prevented Pérez Esquivel from entering; but many observers, photographers, and supporters were able to get to the Plaza by using the subway passage.

Once there, we were able to concretize our desires. By walking for twenty-four hours without stopping, we would certainly get at long last an answer about our children's fate—children who, at that moment, most of us assumed were still alive.

The hours kept going by with different colorations and almost without incident and with the solidarity of the rest of the human rights organizations, which, in addition to accompanying us, brought us food and drink; this even included a solitary inhabitant from nearby who stayed up all night so that we could use the sanitary facilities in his garage.

From this distant perspective, I can remember the loneliness that surrounded us on that famous night of December 11, 1981. Had we analyzed the Plaza's geography correctly? During the day, from eight o'clock a.m. and even more noticeably, towards noon, the Plaza and its surroundings resemble beehive. Thousands of people come and go, criss-crossing each other.

After five p.m., it starts slowly turning into a deserted territory. At the very least, we could have been arrested without any witnesses.

After midnight, Hebe announced: "We have completed one more hour of our march," which provoked sustained applause that gave us renewed energy. For us it meant the realization of one more act of desperate protest—something mysterious that in some way would get us a little closer to our children and which gave us a few hours of calm for our anxiety.

We formed a tight circle of heartbeats and longings which started to spread out with a slow rhythm, they expanded during the evening hours, and finally became tighter again towards the hours of night. The march continued without interruption. Those Mothers who became exhausted would leave while other ones replaced them. Of course the circle became much smaller towards dawn, and we saw the dawn from that circle. And it became even smaller during the early hours of the morning, when we started to feel cold. We were few and there were still so many more hours to go. But with its first newscast a radio announced: "At this very moment, the Mothers are marching around the pyramid." And this acted as a summons for other Mothers and for countless other people to come to the Plaza. And the circle was nourished and became revitalized with noise and energy.

But sadly, this march, conceived as a single protest, has had to be repeated year after year as a symbolic protest until this very day.

The second March of Resistance (December, 1982) had many more incidents, but also larger repercussions.

WITHOUT GIVING UP OUR SPACE

December 1, 1982: "Over a thousand people at the intersection of Avenida de Mayo and Peru carried out the 'March of Resistance.' They defied the hostility of the Federal Police, who prevented the demonstration from taking place at the Plaza de Mayo as originally planned." (*Diario Popular*)

From before four in the afternoon, we were forced to carry out the second March of Resistance along Avenida de Mayo. We Mothers tried hard to break through the circle of police, but failed. Mounted police swarmed on the sidewalks to help other policemen armed with rifles and automatic pistols. Faced with the impossibility of reaching the Plaza, we were forced to hold that week's Thursday circle on the Avenida de Mayo, tying it to the twenty-four hour march.

The dictatorship stubbornly decided to prevent our second march, but we Mothers kept up a dramatic fight by pushing on to reach our Plaza. Finally, lacking any other solution, we spontaneously decided to carry the march out onto the avenue, so that we collided again and again with the circle of police while we shouted: "Freedom, freedom" and "Tell us where the disappeared are."

What had started out with many incidents, acts of repression, and anguish changed from one minute to the next into an intensely fervent march of resistance with uninterrupted singing and with support from all passersby—who applauded—and this included the help of bar owners, who decided to shut their doors for the entire night while placing their tables on the sidewalk. Many of them served us drinks and food without charge.

We organized the third March of Resistance to coincide with Students' Day: from the evening of September 21 to the 22nd, 1983. We were accompanied by a new symbol, thanks to the creativity of three people in the fine arts.

SILHOUETTES: THEY EMERGE FROM OUR DREAMS AND FLOOD THE CITY.

We are at the Plaza. Some of the Mothers approach us and say: "We have to form groups of three or four Mothers to accompany the kids who are carrying buckets of glue to stick the silhouettes on the walls around the Plaza."

At that moment we were with some boys who had volunteered their time and help for this new form of protest.

The idea of drawing faceless silhouettes of the disappeared was the inspiration of a group of people who wanted to loudly voice their pain and opposition about the drama of the disappeared. The way they thought of expressing themselves was with their drawings.

The group of artists who originated the project, Rodolfo Aguerreberry, Julio Flores, and Guillermo Kexel, wanted to produce a social happening by presenting their work at a foundation which exhibited objects and created happenings. But it was too huge a project, the thirty thousand silhouettes could not possibly fit in a salon.

The idea of offering the project to the Mothers of the Plaza de Mayo came up. The Mothers approved it and undertook the financing, together with the Grandmothers, incorporating it to the March of Resistance, which was being organized at that time.

The artists took the material to the Plaza de Mayo: rolls of paper, paint, rollers and cardboard cutouts with the silhouettes of a man, a woman, a child in their natural size.

On September 21, when that march of resistance started, kids from student centers as well as independent militants—hundreds of persons who joined in the task—came to the Plaza. Workshops that went on for twenty-four hours were organized around the pyramid. All of a sudden I found myself on my knees on the ground passionately desiring to make figures. It was a feverish and contagious activity.

When I first saw those silhouettes, I remembered the paper dolls that I used to make for my disappeared daughter. When she was little, she used to wait eagerly to see how the magic of folding and a scissors turned a plain sheet of paper into enchanting creatures, all holding hands. The silhouettes that these boys proposed mixed with my remembrances and at the same time conjured up the mystery of those kids who were missing, but who for a moment gained life and even seemed to come back just to be with us. As if they had really reappeared.

It has already started to get dark. The wind sweeps away lots of paper. Like a hive of bees, hundreds of young people busy themselves among cans of paint, brushes, and rollers. The most enthusiastic ones are covered with paint from head to toe. I thrill to their presence.

The night progresses. There is much coming and going, the movement doesn't stop, and when the sky starts to fill with swatches of red, the first timid lights allow me to discover that again our children have come near. There they are by each tree, each column, by the pyramid, on the Cathedral walls and even beyond, penetrating all the streets of the city. And there is nobody who can fail to recognize them.

They are unavoidable, they come back and come back again. At this moment I am happy. One after the other, the silhouettes of those children for whose return I am always waiting, begin to appear.

A little while later, I finally meet Guillermo, one of the authors of the idea. And I asked him to put in writing the feelings that led him to imagine this way of bringing back the disappeared for a while. And he handed me this text:

FROM THE WALL THOUSANDS OF ABSENTEES DEMAND JUSTICE

"A tacit agreement of silence oppressed millions of people. Fear, hopelessness, confusion turned these people into puppets that moved and spoke as if nothing had happened. Expert illusion-makers were making truth a lie and a lie truth. People looked the other way, smiled while they hurt. And it did hurt.

"And the emptiness and the lie grew. And one day the people screamed silhouettes.

131

"The silhouettes didn't fill the emptiness, they only gave it shape. And quantity. Thousands of people made thousands of silhouettes of thousands of people. Placed the bodies, multiplying them so that they would be inhabited by those who had been kidnapped but still were there. Like an unfamiliar identity rite (they gave back their identities to them, but I am still bleeding inside). They drew what had once existed and then pasted it on the wall.

"The scene on the following day:

"The puppets that we had been could no longer walk through our city as if nothing had happened. Thousands of the missing were demonstrating, demanding justice. Thousands of women and men and kids and the newborn and those not yet born, stood fiercely upright, accusing the torturers, the assassins, the corrupt, those who today still spit in our faces, demanding, threatening, a shameful forgetfulness.

"These silhouettes, these pieces of painted paper, were charged forever with the dignity of the many thousands of men and women who stained their fingers with ink and their clothes with glue in order to make them stand up again.

"The disappeared. Wherever they might be, they haven't stopped struggling for a minute. They are more alive than us."

That same year, a few days after Alfonsín assumed power, we carried out the fourth March of Resistance.

WE THOUGHT IT WOULD BE
THE LAST ONE

On December 8, 1983, almost thirty thousand people congregated in order to accompany us to the Plaza of the Two Congresses. In this crowd we had representatives from Brasil, Uruguay, Bolivia, Paraguay, Chile and Peru. We also had Mrs. Patricia Derian, a former official of President

Carter's administration. Her presence was very much appreciated. She said: "There is no way to describe my own sense of happiness at participating in the last of the marches of the Mothers of the Plaza de Mayo under the military government."

And she added emotionally: "This march is taking place because there have been people willing to risk their lives for their families, for freedom, and especially for justice." A group of newspapermen formed a column carrying posters identifying disappeared colleagues.

At long last the ominous era of the "process" was coming to its end, and we really believed that all of us without any exceptions were going to receive news about our children, but THIS WAS NOT TO BE.

THEY ARE NOT JUST PHOTOGRAPHS: THEY ARE OUR CHILDREN'S FACES.

This "March of the Posters," though not one of the so-called Marches of Resistance, had great emotional significance for me.

We started from Uruguay Street, where the Mothers' residence had first been located. The apartment was small and the elevator practically unusable, so that we went down the stairs almost in the dark. We were a whole bunch of Mothers, each one carrying a poster with a hugely enlarged photograph of her disappeared child, and the name, age and date of disappearance. We waited on the sidewalk, formed in columns. Many young people accompanied us, also carrying photographs. We were ready to start the march. It was the first time that our kids had come out in the streets with us to march since their disappearance.

While we were waiting we held the posters high so that over our heads beautiful faces appeared, youthful, full of life: our children's faces. And how did people passing by us react?

At first surprised, dumbfounded, they stopped. Their eyes remained fixed on the eyes in the photos; the posters remained immobile; immobile also the faces of the passersby. They looked at each other. Because the photos were not simply portraits. They demonstrated an unquestionable existence that had to be restored. Here they were—with these very faces, this is the way they were—with these looks, these expressions, and these poses.

Once the first moments of consternation were over, people commented, pointed, questioned themselves aloud: "But these kids—are they the disappeared? How is this possible?"

I believe that for the first time our children's strong presence—which we feel all the time—was shared by the rest of the people.

Moments before we started marching, I saw coming toward me a young man I had difficulty recognizing. He was one of Graciela's fellow students in college. He embraced me. Very moved, he told me: "I left my office, I saw the photos and from a block away I made out Graciela's. I had to run and give you a hug." I felt deeply touched.

By coming out with the photographs and seeing people's reactions, I understood that we were showing our countrymen the dreadful truth the dictatorship took pains to hide in thousands of ways.

So it was that our disappeared went around the city center awakening the same emotions in everybody they encountered.

The second time we went out with the posters something very singular happened. On arriving in the Plaza de Mayo, we Mothers were surprised by a very big storm. We had already placed ourselves across from the entrance door to the presidential palace. A wall of men in uniform displayed themselves along the whole width of the street. It looked as if they wanted to protect the Pink House from an invasion of all our defiant faces.

The rain was falling hard. In order to protect the photographs, some of the Mothers took refuge in the Ministry's entrance. But many of the older ones, the more hardened ones, stayed in the Plaza in spite of the storm. And there the miracle occurred. The uniformed men did not move from their places. Undoubtedly they were waiting to see the portraits disintegrate and the Mothers disband. On the contrary, the Mothers stayed on without giving up one inch of their Plaza, and from their portraits their children continued to outface them, indestructible in spite of the deluge. One group watched the other. From some of the photos, the smiling faces appeared to defy such a show of authoritarianism.

THERE WAS ALWAYS A SONG...A POEM

I can't remember what year it was, perhaps 1981.

We old-timers were told that the singer Joan Baez wanted to sing for us. In private and specially for us.

We met in a small room at Familiares. We sat in seats as if we were in a theatre. She climbed on a desk and faced us. She sat with her legs gathered up, cross-legged and her guitar held in bandolier fashion.

I remember her face very well, somewhat Indian, dark hair resting on her shoulders, and her hands, very thin and long-fingered. Fingers like fine tubes.

She offered us many songs in her beautiful voice, with her whole body, with all her skin. At times she asked us to accompany her in her singing. We were very moved.

She said that she was sorry for moving us and making us cry.

We told her that crying was good for us and that we needed to cry together, all of us.

It was an unforgettable encounter.... We were in front of somebody who accompanied us, soothed us, loved us....

135

Later I learnt what she said about this experience.

"Oh God! I have never seen so much pain, so much sadness and so much strength all at the same time!"

During those years of horror, greeted in our actions by insults and injuries, we never lacked for a song, a poem, or a guitar. Nostalgically we have even heard snatches of accordion music. It followed us very nearby: it is the people's poetry, which can never be silenced. There is NO repression that can silence it.

Songs and poetry grew wild, rough and strong, because we watered them with our tears. And we were the ones who first began to sing them.

Our thanks go to those artists like María Elena Walsh, Juan Carlos Baglietto, León Gieco, Victor Heredia, Joan Manuel Serrat, Teresa Parodi, Mercedes Sosa, Antonio Tarragó Ross and so many others it hurts not to be able to name, but we feel a surge of love when we remember them.

TESTIMONIES

You with the photo camera,
you wearing the uniform,
do you have any children?
Do you have children named like bells?
Me?
I don't know
I don't know
That's why I stay in the circle.

CARMEN AGUIAR DE LAPACO
mother of
ALEJANDRA MÓNICA LAPACO
abducted on March 17, 1977 at 19 years of age

(Carmen's mother, Carmen Mungos de Aguiar, lived until she was 93 years old and accompanied her daughter in this search).

My daughter was abducted on March 17, 1977.

I am going to tell you a bit about my life, about our lives. When my husband was alive, my house was a very happy place. We were always joking, we even had a private way of talking, changing the words, or saying them backwards.

My husband always used to say: "In this house there is no money, but there is a lot of laughter." You know that in the home of a newspaper man and a school teacher, there can't be much money. It was a home open to everybody. My husband's friends, my friends came; and when Alejandrita started to be of an age to have young friends, we were always ready for them to come to play with her.

My family came from the province of San Juan. My father was of Spanish descent, his family came during colonial times and he belonged to a traditional San Juan family. My mother descended from French immigrants.

The loss of a child

I grew up in a home—let's say Catholic—because often even when one does not practice any religion, one inherits it. And my husband came from a Jewish home, though neither of us practiced our inherited faiths.

Alejandrita grew up in an atmosphere of good treatment and good manners. Quantitatively, I was not able to

138

be with her all of the time I should have been, but it was made up for by my giving her quality attention. Because I had to go out to work, she stayed with my mother, who brought her up from the time she was a baby. When my father died, Alejandra was eight months old and my mother came to live with us. But in fact, the time I devoted to her was really intense, so much so that my husband would tell me: "I don't understand why you have so much to say to each other, so much to talk about." And I would answer: "Maybe you think it is not important, but for her it is. Her friend stole her eraser—her fellow student...!"

So that from the time she was very young, we were very close friends, talked a lot and exchanged confidences.

I don't know whether it was because both my husband and I were big readers, but from the time she was very young she was very interested in everything that had to do with reading, music, art. We sent her to the Colegium Musicum when very young and, and as an adolescent, she began to learn drawing and painting. Unfortunately, she lost her father when she was fifteen years old. That was one of the great losses in her life, and it affected her very deeply. It was the first time I had to send her to a psychologist. Naturally, I was also deeply affected by the loss of my companion. But then I have come to believe that although the loss of one's companion is immense, the loss of one's child is so much greater, something one can never accept. And if parents cannot find consolation when their children die accidentally, it is even harder when it happens the way this has happened.

She was very intelligent. She graduated from secondary school when she was sixteen years old, I mean, she finished her secondary education before the usual age, and immediately entered the University to study Anthropology. She always felt very sorry for the poor; I remember that as a child she used to say: "Ah, Mom! Why are the Three Kings so naughty? They bring nice things to people who have money, and they don't bring anything to the poor children." That's to say, already when very young, she intuitively understood injustice.

On my father's side, we came from a family of politicians. My father was a representative. Politics is one of my family's careers, so that at home Alejandra was fulfilling her part.

When she started college, her militancy in the Peronist Youth movement began, but it was the militancy of a young person, a young person who is just starting out. I would have liked to say that my daughter was a leader, somebody really important, but because of her age, nineteen, unfortunately I can't say that, since she did have some uneasiness while in the Peronist Youth Movement.

It was 11:30 p.m on March 16, 1977. The Combined Forces arrived at our house, entered violently, and after remaining for a few hours—till 2:30 a.m. of the 17th—they took my daughter, her boyfriend, a nephew who was at home, and me to a place that I later found out was the Athletic Club (one of the clandestine places of detention).

My nephew and I were there for two days, but my daughter and her boyfriend remain disappeared. It was a place for torture, blows, a hell.

When we were at home and they asked me why I had books by Jewish writers, why I had Jewish names in my appointment book, and when I told them that was my husband's background, they started to treat my daughter more brutally. They'd say to her: "Jewess, we are going to make soap out of you," etc.

They ask me to give my testimony

After I came out of that hell, the first thing I did—following someone's recommendation—was to go to a lawyer to file a writ of habeas corpus asking for my daughter. This lawyer wanted to charge me so much money—I don't remember the amount now—but I know that with that money I could have bought myself an apartment. When I told him that it was completely impossible for me to pay so much, he told me: "Well, Señora, you can do it by yourself. Go to the Court House and they will show you how..." when he saw I could not provide him with the money.... Later on, I learned that in order to present a "habeas corpus," a lawyer isn't necessary, and also, about the number of lawyers who have disappeared because of their having presented writs of habeas corpus, and for defending political prisoners.

I presented the "habeas corpus," which grew to eight or ten more as time went on without Alejandrita appearing. I addressed myself by letter to Massera, Videla, and to Agosti. The only one who answered was Massera—by phone—because I was giving out my phone number in case they didn't answer in writing, and he gave me an appointment. One of his secretaries, Captain of the Navy González, received me. I saw the letter I had sent, which had been underlined. And he told me that if my daughter was not guilty of anything, in three months she would reappear ringing my doorbell. And if my daughter was guilty of something, in three months I would be told which prison she was being held in. Horrified, I said: "How can a mother live for three months without knowing anything about her daughter?" (So you see, he said three months, and now it's going to be ten years and I'm still alive.) And he responded: "Because if people are told beforehand, they start pestering us with lawyers."

Another thing they told me at that time was to check the Army because they themselves (the Navy people) were honorable men and were not holding anybody. And if I checked with the army for her, surely I would find her. That's to say, they passed the buck among themselves.

141

I started to go to a psychologist because I couldn't see anything. It was as if I were blind. I would put on my glasses and they would become wet. When I began to see the psychologist, she made me cry. I cried and I started to see again. And she told me that what was preventing me from seeing were the tears, that they were blotting out my vision.

From the time all this occurred I had been unable to cry. I was in a state of drowsiness, but not tears, I could not squeeze them out, they would not come out. My mother helped me a lot, because I had to start working. I was walking around like a zombie—because I had to work. And when I'd get home, it was to get into bed and look at the ceiling. Later, my mother would help me go to the Ministry of the Interior.... Because that's where I got the first news about a group of women who were meeting. I found out at the Ministry of the Interior when it was still located in the Government House. I had gone to conduct some business, and a woman also waiting there said: "I want to see if these people will give us an answer: they'd answer us if a group of women met at the Plaza de Mayo and assaulted the Government House." Then I answered: "Yes, but they'd kill us all." "No," she says, "They're not going to kill you." Then a woman next to me tells me that this woman was Irma Roy, the wife of Osvaldo Papaleo, who had disappeared recently. Then another woman said that the Mothers met at the Cathedral. Actually at that time one didn't say Mothers, but "there is a group of women who meet at the Cathedral." We couldn't confirm this, because others said it wasn't so. A few days later, my mother, who was the one friend I had by my side and who helped me in everything (at 72 years of age she was a militant young person looking for her granddaughter) went to the Home Ministry and heard again that there was a group of women meeting at the Cathedral. She went there and didn't find them but practically forced me to go. I didn't find anybody at the Cathedral, but passing by the Plaza de Mayo I saw women sitting. This was at the beginning of the Mothers' meetings when it was still barely a group that sat by the flower beds, or on the benches—the round ones at the Plaza. I stopped nearby and they immediately asked me to give them my testimony.

It was at this moment that somebody explained to me that I should give them a written testimony explaining all that had happened.

At that time, to bring it seemed to me very strange. The first person who approached me and talked with me at length was Tita Maratea. From the beginning Tita and I got to know each other there at the Plaza, and we have kept up the friendship over the years.

When Patricia Derian arrived in Argentina, I read about it in the newspaper and I went to the Plaza to say that we had to ask for an interview, but everybody had already had the same thought. María Adela, Juanita, and I went. We arrived at the United States Embassy, asked for an interview, left our phone numbers so they could call any of us, and each of us returned to our houses. On the following day, I received a call from the Embassy confirming the day and time of the interview with Patricia Derian. After I hung up, I realized that I didn't know the telephone numbers of the two other companions with whom I had gone. And now how could I let them know? And I don't know in which hidden corner of my memory I retained the phone number that Juanita had given out. (Because I knew neither Juanita's nor Adela's last names, it was impossible for me to look them up in the phone book.) So I dialed that phone number, and in fact it was Juanita. I am still asking myself who enlightened me on that day so that I could remember that number. And so we had the interview with Patricia Derian. She was very positive. She already knew a lot of what was happening in Argentina. She listened to our stories. When we started this struggle, people were always interested in our own stories. So we would tell our own experiences and then we would say that in reality the same thing was happening to many other people.

At the Embassy, they were so afraid for us to leave for fear of what might happen to us that they took us in an Embassy car to Plaza Italia and saw that each of us got on a bus.

By telling you this I want to let you see that they already knew what was going on here. Afterwards, my trips to the Plaza became routine. For me, it was as if I found in those people what I could not find in anyone else. We spoke the same language, we understood each other, we shared the same problems. It wasn't that we were masochistic, it was that in facing the same problems, we thought about ways of fighting; we would think of what to do. For instance we could all go and line up at the Court House to present a "habeas corpus" so that they could see there were a lot of us, or we could all line up at the Home Ministry. I mean, these minor things at that time were very important because it was a fight against the dictatorship and against its repression. It wasn't even so simple to march around in our circle at the Plaza. The police surrounded us, they pushed us, they treated us as if we were nothing. Many times they tried to get us out of there. We would go by way of one flower bed, then another one, we would walk around the Plaza on the outside. I mean, we would do everything that we thought in our innocence represented a protest. But we never thought that we were going to turn into what later became the Mothers of the Plaza de Mayo.

Around the world

We were already forming a group, and I marvel about having been one of the first in it because I was excessively shy and I had trouble doing things. Once what happened to my daughter had occurred, it was as if I had awakened, and for her sake I would do anything, and I forgot about my shyness. I may have gone on stammering, I may have spoken in any old way, but I got fully in the fray. And a group of ten or twelve started to meet, sometimes at the Zoo, other times at the Botanical Gardens, and then, when we got to know each other better, at family homes. Of course, we knew that the phones were tapped and we wanted to use a code so that they wouldn't find out which house we were going to meet in. We had agreed on names of hotels or tea rooms—to say "we are going to meet for tea at the Sheraton," for instance, or at any of those places; but our naivete was such that there was always somebody who would suddenly pop up and say: "Is the Sheraton so-and-so's house?"

Our codes didn't last long. What happened is that we started to live clandestinely, because we were very frightened of being taken away, of something happening to us, especially after what happened to Azucena. Azucena Villaflor de Devincenti was one of the first.

I am especially fond of Azucena because she was a person who gave me support from the beginning, and I want to stress this fact. I'll never forget that one day they were talking about their grandchildren, and I started to cry and said: "There is something I will never have—and that will be grandchildren." And she hugged me and started to cry with me.

As I was telling you, we started to get more organized. And in 1979, when the OAS came, they advised us that we should become an association formally so as to be received as a group. And that was how the Association of the Mothers of the Plaza de Mayo was born—with twenty members. Our searching continued, and many mothers were justifiably afraid; they didn't want to give their names. And that can't be criticized because those of us who lived during the period knew what we had exposed ourselves to. I was not risking anything because I had lost all I had, so that I threw myself into all of it because I knew that if I didn't recover my daughter, it was to be loneliness for me. And as you see, I am now alone. And we formed an association and we started to work on our presentation for the OAS. And the proof is that we were received by the OAS as the group of the Mothers of the Plaza de Mayo. Before the OAS came, we had gone to Mexico because the Pope went to Puebla. At that point Elida, Marta, María Adela, Nora, and I went. After Puebla, María Adela, Nora, and I were invited to go to Washington. I have to tell you that all our expenses were covered for those trips. In Washington, they gave us lodgings, because there they were very interested in our meeting with the people from the OAS who were preparing a trip to Argentina.

As I remember it, those of us who traveled first—when it was a true feat to leave the country—were Hebe, María del Rosario, Chela, and Elida. They went to Washington first, then to Italy, back to Washington and then back to Argentina.

In Washington we had many interviews. We met with Patricia Derian at the White House, with many congressmen at the Congress, with Kennedy and others, and also with people from the OAS, who took the subject very seriously. These people saw us several times. They came to Argentina; then they went to Bolivia to present the conclusions they had gotten after a visit to Uruguay—but they also mentioned the Argentinian problem. Then Hebe, Elida and I traveled to Venezuela to present the problem there. We were already thinking that we had to make the whole world know; that was the object of our trips. The pressure that we could exercise here was minuscule, and we thought that if the world heard from our own mouths what was going on here, maybe some pressure would be put on the Argentinian government. I want to tell you that we learned more about what was going on when we were outside Argentina than we knew here, because you can be sure the press didn't say anything, and because of fear people whispered only, but there was no talking about this matter out in the open or clearly.

Rabbi Rosenthal from the Jewish Movement received us in New York. He was a very understanding man and he explained to us that he was not petitioning for Jewish people only, but for all the cases which were brought to him, whether they were Jewish or not.

Afterwards, in 1981, we traveled to Europe with María Adela, first to Spain, because the parliament was meeting. And from Spain we were invited to go to other places. We were also guests of the French government; we went to the European Parliament and there we met Simone Weil, who had been a Nazi prisoner. She still had the tattooed number from the concentration camp, and she told us that she understood us fully. Several of the European parliamentarians received us and listened to us.

After our stay in France, which I can tell you was very enriching, we were invited by Germany. We covered it from North to South and from East to West in such a way that we would arrive in a town where we would stay for one or two days, then be taken to a train, from which we were immediately received by another town. It was very important, because people showed great interest. I remember that we met in a church where there was a group of women, all of them knitting, which made me feel bad. They were going to listen to the things we had to say and they were knitting. At a given moment, I realized that while I was talking, they were crying. And being all grown women, elderly, suddenly one of them said: "It is a repetition of what happened here in Germany, what happened under Hitler." So I then realized that what I took for lack of interest is just a habit of theirs, because at several other meetings, the same thing happened. But those women impressed me, crying and remembering their past.

I could not stop fighting

Now I would like to talk a little about Alejandra, to tell you what Alejandra was like. I have already told you about the good relationship we enjoyed from the time she was very young.

I remember that once the fourth grade teacher asked each girl what they were going to be when they grew up. When she got to Alejandra, she said to her: "I am not going to ask you because I already know what. You are going to be a writer." She had a talent for writing and at that age she was already writing poems. But when she became an adolescent, she loved music a lot, she played the guitar and sang. She had graduated as an elementary school French teacher and worked at a French nursery school, the Jean Mermoz, as a teacher. But afterwards, when she was about to finish high school, she devoted herself exclusively to painting. I have a painting that awakens a lot of pain in me, and I try to hide it. She painted it after her father's death, and in that painting, which she called "You are resting in profound peace," she reveals all the pain she felt.

I knew of her political militancy. We shared a lot together, almost everything. Sometimes we would get into discussions, but we did it in an open manner, that's to say, in a clear way, without reproach. Perhaps I failed to convince her of what I saw as wrong, and maybe she didn't convince me about what she wanted to do, but we did not avoid talking about the subject. I still remember how on the evening she was abducted I didn't talk to her, but to Marcelo. I said that these were moments when they should perhaps step backwards, so as to be able later to step forwards, to withdraw a bit from their activities, the political fray. They were youngsters at the time, so it wasn't an armed fight, but a fight of political ideas.

Alejandra was very pretty. She was more or less as tall as I am, five feet, four inches, with dark hair and green eyes which when she became annoyed, turned dark green. I mean, they changed with her moods, and sometimes they'd become grey. She was a girl with a lovely figure, but above all she was more beautiful inside than outside. I know it's said that mothers never find defects in their children. Yes, she had all the defects and all the qualities that a human being has. But in spite of the fact that she had been an only child, everybody would tell me that we had not spoiled her. At this moment, I am sorry, I feel we should have pampered her a bit more; but our fear that as an only child she would become whimsical and willful made us act a bit severely so that she would see things clearly.

She began to work while quite young. When she was fifteen, her father gave her a job at his office, and she used to go for one or two hours to help him, to answer the phone and to take messages.

As I told you, after that, she became a teacher at the Jean Mermoz school. Then she worked at the Alejandro Korn Publishing House, and that day, on the morning of the day of her disappearance, she asked me to go to the University to look for some papers because she was working and had to prepare a subject for an examination. I went and I took these papers directly to the publisher's. At that very moment, while I was there at the publisher's, the principal of the Jean Mermoz School called to ask her to go back to the school to teach.

I mean she was responsible, very responsible about her work. The proof is that they were calling her back, and she was only nineteen years old. In her studies she got very good marks. On that fateful day, when they came to our house to look for her, she had planned to go to a fellow student's house to study and wasn't going to be at home. But the exam was moved forward—instead of Friday, now it was going to be on Monday. Logically enough, she decided not to go to study with a school friend since she had already prepared the subject, and she could study on

Saturday and Sunday and take the examination on Monday. I recall that I became annoyed and said to her: "But Alejandra, how come you're not going to your friend's when you had agreed to do so?" "But Mother, I already have the subject down pat, what are you thinking of? Do you think I'm not going to be prepared?" Ah! one thing she used to say to me: "I'm studying what I like, and what I like I want to know. I don't study as an obligation. I study because I like to study." And I remember that on that evening I said to Marcelo, Alejandra's boyfriend: "Marcelo, go on, leave!" And he replied: "You're jealous, you want me to leave because you don't want me to be with your daughter...." But I had never told them any such thing, and on that very day there I was quarreling with them. I don't know, it might have just been chance or I don't know what. I always wanted the kids to be at home, but on that evening, I was practically pushing them out.

Now I'm going to tell you about the feelings I experienced when I'd go to bed after Alejandrita's disappearance. We had a certain form of communication, something so intangible that it's difficult to explain, but it was as if my thoughts and hers were meeting and we were united; but after about two months, all communication with Alejandra was cut off. It was a very odd feeling, it can't be explained.

I could have dreamt about her. I've had dreams...for instance, I once dreamt that she and my husband were on a very, very high place, and that I was climbing up a staircase without ever being able to reach the place where they were. I would keep climbing, climbing. The dream kept repeating itself.

Afterwards, during those years of struggle, while I was learning more about the things around us, or about myself in particular, I had the feeling that the kids were not alive. But at the bottom of her heart and against all hopelessness, a mother keeps on thinking: "Perhaps my daughter is still alive, she found somebody who protected her. Yes, there might be many dead, but they couldn't have killed them all. Some have to be alive." I mean that in spite of the evidence that told about their being dead, as a mother I didn't want to accept it.

Later, I thought that even if my daughter were dead, I could not stop fighting for those kids, not only for my daughter, but for all the kids. First, because we were not giving my daughter and all those kids away as gifts to anybody. It had to be us who would vindicate their struggles, their ideals. And then, because we must also believe they gave of themselves, body and soul, knowingly—because they knew what they were exposing themselves to. But in spite of this they gave their young blood for their ideals. We, the people who had given them birth—weren't we going to give all we had so that all this would not be forgotten? So that the guilty are punished. It's true that now there are many things which don't please us. But there are many other things that have allowed us to see that the fight's not been in vain. Because we have been able to seat on the bench of the accused a great number of those arrogant men, though not all of them.

Maybe the person who killed my daughter won't be judged in my daughter's case, but it's possible that he'll be judged in others'. And this, I believe, was worth our fight. And I believe that, in spite of the fact that they want to put an end to all this, for us there won't be an end. We are going to keep on in every possible way, because there are many ways for us to keep on being the living memory of what has happened.

CARMEN ISABEL RODINO DE COBO
mother of
INÉS ADRIANA COBO
abducted when 22 years old
on September 1, 1976

The abduction

My case starts from the moment of the abduction of my
older daughter, Inés Adriana Cobo, on September 1st,
1976. We were living at that time in this house, with my
husband, my younger daughter, my older one, my father,
and myself, five very happy people. That's when our
family's other story begins, another manner of living,
another manner of focusing our existence: the rhythm of
life that we all came to live.

My husband is of Spanish descent and my background's Italian. At the time of the abduction, my older
daughter was working with her father while the younger
one had just entered the University to study biology. My
husband worked as a newspaperman for a specialized
magazine and I worked as a grammar school teacher. I say
that our life changed so much because, a short time later, I
left my teaching activities to devote myself entirely to the
search for Inés, my disappeared daughter. I cannot describe
the abduction because it happened on the street. We don't
know what happened, who abducted her, under what
circumstances, or the people who were involved in it. As to
the time of the abduction, we guess it could have been at
1:20 p.m. on the above-mentioned day, within an area
which could have been situated between Pueyrredón and
Peña Streets and the Children's Hospital, which was where
my daughter was going.

At that time, of course, there were entities devoted to
the defense of human rights, like the Argentinian League

for the Rights of Men, the Permanent Assembly for Human Rights, and the Ecumenical Movement for Human Rights. But as of yet there existed no entities created by the families of the victims, as for instance the Mothers, Relatives, and Grandmothers. Of course, we appealed to the entities in operation. But the fact is that we, the affected parties, would congregate frequently in public places, where we'd go to seek out information about our children (we used to meet at church porticos or at our houses, to exchange information, points of view, doubts, heartbreaks, and to see what else we could do). Little by little, this gave place to the forming of groups of the affected relatives. Thus it was that the Relatives of the Detained-Disappeared for Political Reasons, Mothers of the Plaza de Mayo, and Grandmothers of the Plaza de Mayo came into being.

I became part of the Mothers' organization as a consequence of the searches and the work that we were carrying out individually and collectively. This entity was formed many months after my daughter's disappearance, so that it really started forming at the same time we were carrying out the search for our children. Not only did I get close to the Mothers, I also got close to the Relatives of the Detained-Disappeared. Among the procedures we undertook were those concerning "habeas corpus" presentations before the authorities, formal complaints to the ministries, etc. In addition, we tried to form a core group because we felt our load became lighter when we could talk about our children. We felt understood; it was a feeling that we all shared. We used to talk about what our loved ones were like, about their hopes, their ideals.

Remembering her as she was the last time I saw her

At the time they took her away Inés was twenty-two years old. She had started studying psychology at the University.

But at this point she had suspended her studies because the field of study had been suspended for two years. She was working as a publicist at the same office as her father. Physically she was a slender young woman, of medium height, dark brown hair, coffee-colored eyes, very pretty, perhaps a bit shy, very humble, without great concern about her personal appearance. She dressed simply and didn't use makeup.

She would become especially distressed when she saw children suffering, and not only her country's children, but those anywhere in the world. This was almost an obsession. She thought that total justice would only be achieved when all the children in the world could have a childhood.

She was very preoccupied with this, and her fellow students and friends shared her thoughts.

A short time after Inés' disappearance, another episode that deeply affected us took place. And that was the abduction of Noemí, my younger daughter. This abduction only lasted twenty-four hours, but it was enough to cause our total unhinging. Because on that day both of our daughters disappeared. Then Noemí reappeared spontaneously, but after a little while, she was detained again and remained out of reach for sixteen days, during which time we didn't know whether she was being held in detention or not, because they denied us access to her. At the police station where they had her, they denied that she was there. We knew she was there from information we had gathered, but officially they denied she was being detained. After sixteen days, the police chief handed her over without any explanation. From then on, things like this didn't occur again. She kept on with her studies. We suffered great anxiety, because to attend the university during those years was daring. Not withstanding, she insisted on continuing with her studies. It's already been ten years and six months since they took Inés. We haven't had any official response, and I don't know anything about her whereabouts. I have had leads, but we haven't been able to corroborate them. Many times I have thought that if I ever I saw my daughter again by one of those miracles that take place in life sometimes...and, well, I haven't been able to stop remembering her the way she was the last time I saw her, twenty-two years old (now she would be thirty-three), so vigorous, looking hardly eighteen, her small-featured, dear face, and those eyes so full of innocence, and with such an idealistic way of seeing things.

And I don't believe she would have changed. I wish she were the way she was the last time I saw her.

Many people used to say that she had old-fashioned ideas about love. Since she was so reserved, I used to insist that she go out, go to parties with people her age, even that she had to...meet young people from the opposite sex, talk to them, establish a friendship. And I remember that when she was fifteen, she told me: "Look Mom, I wasn't born to be a flirt. The day I go out with a boy, it will be because I'm going to be with him forever, for life, because I don't like to waste my time or make others waste theirs." That's the way she thought when she was fifteen. And she really stuck to it, because when she became twenty, she met Rubén Alberto, the love of her life. I want to leave his name in print (sobbing breaks Carmen's voice) because he was an extraordinary companion, the man who made her happy during the few years he was with us. Rubén Alberto was abducted one year after Inés. When they took her, I begged him to leave the country. I promised him, I swore to him, that if we recovered Inés I would send her to him any place in the world where he was. And his answer was: "Mrs. Cobo: I don't want Inés to think I am a coward. I want her to keep on loving me, and I am going to stay here to look for her together with you, so that she finds me if she comes back." Rubén Alberto, who could have saved himself but who didn't because of his love for my daughter. Rubén Alberto Stockdale, who was abducted on September 3, 1977.

GLADYS CASTRO DE LEPISCOPO
mother of
PABLO LEPISCOPO
disappeared when 24 years old, August 5, 1979

You ask me to write something about my dear disappeared Pablo. "Disappeared," a word that after so much use has lost the sense of the macabre in its meaning.

Pablo grew up in Béccar, one of the towns that forms part of Metropolitan Buenos Aires. In spite of being part of the County of San Isidro, it is a worker's or lower middle class neighborhood. Ten blocks away, there is the "Cava," a "villa miseria" at whose sight even indifferent people shudder.

He was an outstanding student in grammar school. He was not only a good fellow student, but also a good brother and a better son.

I always aspired for him to go to high school at the National High School of Buenos Aires because of the education its students received, and because that school made its students think. That was the beginning of his tragic fate: thinking.

This adolescent started to grow up in a home where we always took note of social injustice. It was also the historic moment when the country stopped looking back at Europe and tried to understand Latin America in its destiny of underdevelopment and misery. Now, thanks to the military governments which were always pressing forward to "save" us, Argentina was becoming like the rest of Latin America.

All of this formed a background to his convictions, and so he started to participate. He didn't want to be an accomplice to the barbarism that was governing us.

The proximity to San Isidro showed you young people whose highest aspirations were to have a motorbike and a high standard of living at any cost, a mirror of that place itself, San Isidro.

Nevertheless, Pablo had experience in factories. He worked as a lathe operator and shared the hard life of the low-salaried with the other workers. On weekends he helped some of them construct their houses.

That life of sacrifice that used to hurt me as a mother is today something that makes me feel proud of my son, who, though lacking the need, was able to understand other people's needs and to try to remedy them.

When my husband and I chose to have children—because it wasn't an accident in our lives—we told each other that there would be two priorities in their education: independence and freedom.

Pablo learnt the lesson because he chose his way.

Facing the pain of his loss, I ask myself what I would change.

And I always end up convinced that the tenderness, sensitivity, and convictions I saw in my son were what I had hoped for in my children.

On August 5, 1979, our family received the hardest and most terrible blow. We narrowed our feelings, first in the search, then in the hope, and finally we arrived at the conviction of the tragedy.

Since then sadness and pain have lodged themselves in our hearts.

Seven years have not been able to heal the wounds. They are the wounds of the injustice, impunity, and cruelty that cut off his life without having allowed him to defend himself, a privilege today allowed his aggressors.

Finally, I want to express my wish that my son, like so many others who have vanished, may have created an opening for a more just, more reflective, and more partici-patory society.

CHAPTER 6

DEMOCRACY ARRIVED

"You Mothers and Grandmothers of the Plaza de Mayo taught us, who thought we had discovered everything, that horror never ceases to widen the limits of the possible. You taught us to listen to the voices of silence in the course of your endless circle."

—Edmond Jouve

(At the closing of the Colloquium at a Convention Against the Disappearances, Buenos Aires, October, 1988).

ONE WAITED FULL OF HOPE

I am not going to keep stressing the anxiety that dominated us as the beginning of our democratic government quickly approached.

Finally the long-awaited day arrived, that day for which we had struggled and marched without rest.

On the morning of December 10, 1983 all the Mothers, every one of us, accompanied by our friends and close relatives and by the other organizations for human rights, placed ourselves across from the Cabildo (the Government House during Colonial times). A few years before, we thought this day would never arrive. With our posters, our flags, our signs, with all our jubilation, we prepared ourselves for our brand new constitutional president's speech.

The people were happy. It was a radiant day, we were leaving behind a long night of anxieties. But very deep in our hearts, we were certain that Dr. Alfonsín was already compromised. Just the same, there was so much to hope for....

We listened attentively to his entire speech. And we remained thirsty for much more action on our claims. Nevertheless, we hid the bitterness that some undefined words produced in us.

But it was a fiesta! Even when two missing groups gave it a tragic tone: the disappeared and the Malvinas kids.

When we broke up along Avenida de Mayo, people recognized us because of our white kerchiefs, and they hugged us, they encouraged us, thinking that soon, very soon, we would have news about our children.

AND WERE THERE STILL
DISAPPEARED ALIVE?

On the same day at the Mothers' Residence, Robert Cox, the newspaperman who had come to attend, implied that there were still people alive in concentration camps very far from Buenos Aires. In addition, we also saw Patricia Derian, who talked to us about her feelings and her happiness at being in Buenos Aires surrounded by the families of the disappeared under a democratic government. She also encouraged us regarding the supposition that there were survivors. Nine months after this date, Pérez Esquivel's declarations about Cecilia Viñas de Perino appeared, a woman who had been abducted and disappeared in 1977 and who, between December 1983 and March 1984, had talked on the phone with her family eight times.

Now that we already had a democratic government, why didn't they put an end to our uncertainties and why did they keep up the leaks and the extra-official messages? Why did the mystery have to continue? Why did the members of the families have to continue to search on their own?

IMAGES BEYOND WORDS

It was Thursday. I don't know whether it was before I went to the Plaza. I saw it on the TV. It was simply horrible. In an excavated plot among lumps of earth, a huge machine like some sort of a crane was digging with its teeth—was enlarging a hole and then heaving out to one side...bones, human bones. We saw tibias, femurs, pelvises, bones of all sizes, white bones.

That is what they wanted to give back to us of our children.

They had not dared to tell us what they had done with our disappeared.

But this was the way they found to lead us to assume that they were no longer alive.

All this was happening at the dawn of democracy, when thousands of Mothers and relatives were rushing forward with demands to let us know our children's whereabouts. Hundreds of lawsuits had been initiated. Many people had received data about their children, who had been seen in clandestine locations.

People were already aware that unidentified persons had been buried in the cemeteries of Boulogne Sur Mer, San Martín, and Avellaneda. In this context—perhaps to make us give up?—those images appeared again and again in the news. They were showing us the horrible drama of the disappeared in the most sadistic and disrespectful way.

I could barely face these images, barely stand to look at them, and yet, frozen and dumb, I could not stop looking at them either.

If what they wanted was to give us an answer that would paralyze us with its horror, they merely succeeded in provoking in us a deep depression and a limitless anxiety.

But they didn't steer us away from our goal: to deepen the investigation of our children's fate and to obtain an answer based on each case, for which the military would assume its responsibility.

WE WOULD DO ANYTHING....

The Mothers received the following information regarding the offices at 1700 Lavalle Street: they were throwing away valises with documents. On the rather cool dawn of September 8, 1984, we Mothers, wearing our white kerchiefs, stood guard, sitting on the threshold of the building at 1700 Lavalle Street. There on the 8th and 9th floors, and perhaps also on the 6th and the 4th, were the offices of the lawyers

Klein and Mairal. Later on, neighbors brought us chairs and coffee.

By morning, we were joined by many more Mothers, Grandmothers, Families, and neighbors, brought by the news on the radio. The night had been rather long, but we had been able to stop more documentation folders from being taken.

What kind of absurdity were the "old women" into instead of staying home taking care of their families? We had received a call reporting that information related to the disappearances and the repression was being kept in some inoffensive-looking offices downtown.

At mid-morning, Klein arrived at his office and there he saw that a delegation from the Mothers of the Plaza de Mayo was waiting for him. Klein, a former secretary for Economic Programs during the dictatorship, talked to some of the Mothers for half an hour. And afterwards, at a press conference, he complained that he was faced with a campaign orchestrated to destroy reputations. Furthermore he said: "The ladies asked me if we had documents related to the disappeared and I told them no, that I don't have any documents regarding this matter, and that I regret all the violence the Republic has suffered." Later on he addressed the National Commission on Missing Persons in writing, inviting the members of the commission to investigate "his personal files exclusively concerning the public operations to which the news makes reference."

Once again, the Mothers, bewildered, had the possibility of almost touching this precious documentation with their own hands, documentation that they had screamed for so many times when they demanded, "What has happened to our children?"

I remember such demands had started a parliamentary investigative commission in which Congressman Tello Rosas took part.

But this investigation, like so many others, melted away. Once again, we remained empty handed.

ALFONSÍN'S CONCESSIONS

I don't want to leave aside any of the measures adopted by Alfonsín's government. They began to undermine our hopes for finding a quick solution and for encountering our disappeared again. I am not going to make a judicial analysis, but I want to comment on what started happening to us so that we began feeling repercussions.

THE BICAMERAL COMMISSION: AN EXERCISE IN FRUSTRATION

Will they or won't they form the Dual Chamber Commission? This was a project that was making its way around the organizations for human rights. They had explained to us that if a commission formed by representatives and senators were created, it would thoroughly investigate and judge the military dictatorship's repressive policies. Who but the representatives and senators, elected by us, would be better to investigate the accusations of the detained-disappeareds' relatives? They would be supported by the full force of the law and all the powers conferred upon them by Congress. Since the issue concerned such a cruel repression, planned and organized beforehand, it was truly for the representatives and senators to investigate and make known the methods used by the dictatorship, not only as crimes against individuals, but as a policy of genocide.

I want to reproduce part of an article published in December, 1983 in *El Porteño*: "The Commission of the Two Chambers,

Why?" by Dr. Conte, a representative in Congress and the father of one of the disappeared.

> *"There are not only substantial ethical problems involved here. There are, besides, criteria of political realism which show that gross social facts inexorably emerge at the foundations of a community, even more so when an effort is made to hide or restrict them. Great pain, great savagery, great inhumanity are latent, so people think that they can be avoided by escapism and superficialities. Let us make clear that the enactment of justice is one thing, and political pronouncements another, each quite different from the other. Justice shows itself by concrete facts and concerns those responsible in particular. Its role is not to pronounce judgment on policies or on global situations. The latter is a function of political bodies, which does not prejudice sending to the Department of justice the facts gathered in the course of the investigation. They carry it out, or it isn't done. It is that simple."*

Unfortunately, this project didn't materialize. Dr. Alfonsín opted for CONADEP (National Commission on Missing Persons).

CONADEP: AN EMERGENCY DOOR

CONADEP was the commission created on December 15, 1983 to inquire about the fate of our disappeared. Its objective was not to investigate the authors of the kidnappings, but to gather accusations and testimonies, and to verify the existence of hundreds of clandestine sites of detention.

This commission did not fulfill our expectations, but nevertheless, it attracted thousands and thousands of fathers, mothers, relatives, and also former detained-disappeared persons, who came to give their testimonies in the hope of helping in the investigation and, furthermore, to complete their own data. Unfortunately—since it was something very horrible—through the jumble of accusations gathered by the National Commission on Missing Persons and then confirmed during the hearings, some of the Mothers learnt that their children had been thrown into the sea from planes after having received an injection. Others got confirmation that their children were still alive until they gave birth while in prison. They did not go on to finish compiling data. The absolute truth has never been made clear.

From the enormous documentation gathered, it became clear that the violation of human rights carried out by the armed forces was systematic: done always in the same manner, with the same sort of abductions, identical kinds of torture in all the territory of the Republic, like a planned-out affair. The military put forward the phony argument that "in every war mistakes and excesses always happen," thus denying their responsibility for the disappearances.

The epilogue to CONADEP's work was the book printed by the University of Buenos Aires Press. It is a thick volume that produced a strong impact on the world's conscience under a title which is itself an ethical scream, "NEVER AGAIN."

This commission revealed and broadcasted the atrocities performed during the decade of the '70s, but it wasn't the right instrument to investigate the crimes thoroughly or to pronounce judgment on the methods used to exercise terror on the Argentinian people, as would have been done by the Two Chambers' Commission, which we advocated.

That is to say, it investigated a lot concerning the disappeared, but it revealed very little about the disappearers.

THE LEGAL PROCESSES AGAINST
THE JUNTAS

On the basis of the documentation obtained by CONADEP, trials of the three first military juntas of the last dictatorship were initiated. Alfonsín decided that the Supreme Council of the Armed Forces should proceed to judge their peers for their involvement in the repression which started with the 1976 military coup. But, as it was to be expected, the Supreme Council did not put any of their peers on trial because it indefinitely delayed taking up their cases. That is why the Government felt obliged to withdraw the cases from the Supreme Council and to pass them on to the federal judiciary. And this is how the spectacularly famous trials, which so moved the Argentinian people, were initiated.

The horror and the cruelty were exposed through a very ample window, since these were conducted as oral and public trials. The trial was filmed, although it was never shown to the Argentinian TV viewers.

This judicial process brought to Buenos Aires many newspaper people from the most important international media.

During a recent interview, one of the participating judges, Dr. Arslanian, acknowledged the tremendous human effort that went into accomplishing the trial of the juntas: "In two weeks, we had to pose twenty-two thousand factual questions that made up the backbone of the final judgment; we also had to consider thousands of acts that were not only cases of homicide but were also cases of illegitimate deprivation of freedom, along with very many other incidental felonies. Then we got substantiating proof by means of complex public and oral hearings, dramatic ones filled with tension."

It was incredibly distressing for us Mothers, who had obtained so much data on our children's fate, to sit on a bench at the hearings and wait for the protagonists under judgment and their judges to reveal once and for all what had been our children's final destiny. Because in addition to anticipating the repressors' sentences, we were hoping to be able to reconstruct the complete web of the mystery that had been with us all these years. In spite of the fact that we finally learnt that the methods used in all the cases were similar, we needed to know concretely what they had done to each one of our children. Nevertheless, only some of the Mothers learned this. The macabre devices used were conceived to prevent our reaching the truth.

Finally, the trial ended with the sentencing of the members of the three first military juntas.

THE STATUTE OF LIMITATIONS: "THE WILL OF SIXTY-THOUSAND WAS NOT ENOUGH."

A very wide column of people walked downtown from the Obelisk on Avenida 9 de Julio, along Corrientes and then Callao, to the Congress. "NO TO THE STATUTE OF LIMITATIONS" was their slogan. The president of the Mothers of the Plaza de Mayo, Hebe de Bonafini, and the Nobel Peace Price winner, Adolfo Pérez Esquivel, headed the column. We had with us some sixty thousand people. This crowd, which filled up about four blocks, was demonstrating against the proposal of the Executive Power to set a conclusion to cases against the military and the civilians implicated in serious violations of human rights.

A few days later, the National Executive Power enacted Law 23.492, called the Law of the Statute of Limitations. This law establishes a sixty day period as the time limit between the law's enactment and any request to make a deposition of inquiry concerning anyone presumed to have participated in crimes against human rights, or to bring new accusations against them. Once this time limit expires, there cannot be any punitive action taken against such a person, with the exception of those cases dealing with the abductions of minors.

What happened in practice, is that the avalanche of cases was such that the judges started to send them out so that they could meet the time requirement. The original idea of cutting off the trials abruptly became obstructed by the number of crimes. And so it was that they had to opt for a new legal sophistry: the Law of Due Obedience (la Ley de Obediencia Debida).

THE LAW OF DUE OBEDIENCE: UNLAWFUL, UNJUST AND UNCONSTITUTIONAL

On June 5, 1987, the text of the Law of Due Obedience approved by the representatives at the Congress appeared in the Buenos Aires newspapers. It declares that "those accused of the felonies referred to by Art.10.1 of the Law # 23.049, 2-13-84, who served as chief officers, sub-officers, petty officers and troop personnel in the Armed Forces, Security, Police or jails at the time of the commission of the deeds, are presumed not punishable, without need to submit proof, because they behaved under the requirement of due obedience." And it continues: "In such cases, it will be considered that the aforementioned persons acted in a state of coercion, under conditions of subordination to superior authority, and followed orders without power, or possibility of consideration, opposition or resistance to them regarding their appropriateness and legitimacy."

I believe it worthwhile to reproduce the words of Dr. Ricardo Molina at the press conference of the American Association of Jurists (6-4-87): "This law of blind obedience is anti-juridical, unjust and unconstitutional. And it is important to expose the existence of a group of robots in

169

Argentinian society who can be sent to perform any aberrant act under orders which up to now do not appear anywhere, and which everybody denies. Besides, this law is useless, because it is not going to solve any problems, since the military sectors will not be satisfied with it because they are actually looking for the vindication and glorification of what has been done, that is to say, of their crimes."

With the promulgation of this Law, they were again demanding that we continue to live with these men who had tortured and abused our children. At the Plaza we Mothers kept up our demands: "No to the final conclusion, no to impunity. Trial and punishment for all guilty parties!"

COSENA AND THE OMNIBUS LAW

One of the last pieces of juridical backsliding relating to how the military could act on questions of internal security consisted of the creation of a Committee of National Security—COSENA—(Alfonsín's Governmental Decree # 327). This legalized the intervention of the Armed Forces in cases of danger to internal security.

Just after this, the government decided to take steps to work on a law they called "omnibus." It would have modified and unified things relating to the defense of internal security. This project meant another big step backwards in the gains that the democratic government had stood for when it began. But it did not become law.

THEY ARE NOT GOING TO DEMOBILIZE US

As the hours moved on, our expectations were quickly being destroyed. Our first frustration was the much in demand Dual Chamber Commission, which was never formed.

CONADEP along with the trials of the first three Military Juntas served to lay bare reality. After that, some advances and much backsliding kept us alert and mobilized. During Alfonsín's whole period, we had to keep up the struggle while facing a self-evident loss of ground for our demands. A series of laws, projects, and decrees exposed the "democratic" government's big surrender in the cause of human rights.

THE FIFTH MARCH OF RESISTANCE

We stepped onto the threshold of democracy, but the fight continues without pause.

The Fifth March of Resistance was organized for December 21, 1984. Again, there was large attendance. We Mothers didn't give up and we gave voice to the slogan: "Trial and punishment for all guilty parties."

As always, present at our march was the Organization for Peace and Justice, headed by Nobel prize winner Adolfo Pérez Esquivel. From the very beginning—the first marches or when we were just getting out into the streets—Adolfo's presence was an invaluable support.

THEY ALWAYS GAVE US A HAND

We spent that evening—the evening before one of the many marches we had organized against the amnesty and the immunity to punishment—by putting up drawings of hands. The many young people who always helped us out assisted. We started at the Congress and continued all the way to the Plaza de Mayo, which we left totally covered with these hands.

Where did this idea come from? We were sent drawings from Holland as a show of love and support. These drawings—of the outlines of female hands done on white

171

paper—bore the written names of Dutch women connected to the campaign of our friends in solidarity, the SAAM women. Because of such a warm gesture, Hebe got the idea of organizing a march with the many, many hands of solidarity all over the world. María Adela went to Cuba to a Congress of the Federation of Cuban Women. There were many women from all over at that occasion. María Adela had taken along printed fliers announcing the march. Naturally, the women wanted to participate, and outlined their hands on papers, so that María Adela came back with an impressive amount; she brought back hands from America, Asia, Europe and Africa. Besides, hands arrived from France, Belgium, Spain—from all over the world. And the hands kept coming in. To be exact, we received hands from eighty-six countries. In addition, the campaign in our country gave us an enormous number of stretched-out hands....

This was one of the marches that moved me the most, a beautiful march, with many participants sharing great solidarity, enthusiasm and overwhelming strength. As we were marching along Avenida de Mayo, the people clapped their hands in unison, making them resound as if they were all one.

I remember the slogan. From the start it made us enthusiastic and moved us because of its effective symbol: a hand has so much meaning: to lend a hand, to give a hand, hand in hand, to join hands. "During the year of the Young...lend a hand to the disappeared."

During the campaign, we placed ourselves at very busy street corners at improvised tables holding a large number of sheets of paper with the printed slogan. After inquiring, everybody who came near offered a hand, which they placed open on a sheet of paper, and we would trace its outline. They would write their names, and most of them also gave the number of their identity document, and many added a phrase of support. We gathered practically one million hands.

Those hands, hanging on cords, were displayed on a very significant day for all of us: March 24, 1985. On that day, it would be nine years since the 1976 military coup.

THE SIXTH MARCH OF RESISTANCE

On December 11, 1985, we carried out the Sixth March of Resistance. Our slogans were: "NO to the Statute of Limitations," "Make them reappear alive," and "Trial and Punishment for all the guilty parties." At dawn we showed several movies on human rights and read poems on the disappeared. Several artists worked with us, encouraging us with their songs and their poems. Many "NO to the Statute of Limitations" signs were painted. And confronted with Dr. Alfonsín's hints about reconciliation, the Mothers responded: "We Mothers don't need to be reconciled with the Argentinian people, we are part of the people and our relationship is a peaceful one. As far as the military and the civilians who committed these perverted crimes are concerned, we declare that there is no possible reconciliation: they must be tried and punished to the full extent of the law."

SEVENTH MARCH OF RESISTANCE

On December 15, 1986, the Seventh March of Resistance, organized against the Statute of Limitations, ended with a demonstration across from the Casa Rosada (Government House) during which six Mothers spoke, among them Hebe de Bonafini.

At about six in the evening, we circled for the last time before forming a column.

173

We felt we were in good company. Prosecutor Molinas spoke: "I would never have been absent from this March at a moment when a proposal for a statute of limitations is being discussed." He got a big ovation.

We were very sorry about the Church's decision to put a fence around the Cathedral steps. But this behavior didn't surprise us. The Church's behavior towards us continued to be hostile.

THE EIGHTH MARCH OF RESISTANCE OR THE MARCH OF THE KERCHIEFS

Thousands and thousands of kerchiefs bearing the legend "Jail for the perpetrators of genocide" were tied all around the Plaza, covered the tops of the trees, hung from the light poles, dressed the bushes and the traditional palm trees, even the pyramid was dressed in white kerchiefs, and amidst all this a big sign rose up that said: "We won't forget, we won't forgive."

Each kerchief represented the support and solidarity of a compatriot or a foreign supporter. Even many days after the march, kerchiefs from all over the world kept arriving.

It was the Eighth March of Resistance, held on December 9, 1987.

THE NINTH MARCH OF RESISTANCE

1988: The Ninth March of Resistance. Twelve years of walking in the circle every Thursday; nine marches of resistance, and still resisting: lack of news, lack of answers, statutes of limitations and owed obediences.

The idea of one single twenty-four hour March of Resistance alone simply wasn't realistic. Regrettably, we had to do it again and again, both under dictatorship and under democracy.

It doesn't matter how long it takes, the idea of demanding truth and justice will keep pushing us on, and we will continue marching until we get an answer.

A DIFFERENT EXPERIENCE: AMNESTY INTERNATIONAL'S ROCK CONCERT

Amnesty International had the brilliant idea of denouncing all the horrendous violations of human rights before the whole world—disappearances, jailings, torture and death—by using the music of the young people. Instead of using their traditional method of communication: sending out huge mailings to put on pressure regarding a certain situation, it got the idea of organizing international tours which would have enormous repercussions on the world's youth. The artists in solidarity who wanted to be part of this experience used all their will power and popularity for this effort in the cause of human rights.

To celebrate the fortieth anniversary of the Declaration of Human Rights, in 1988, Amnesty International organized an international rock concert which traveled through several countries and which gave its final concert in Buenos Aires. Artists as renowned as Sting, Peter Gabriel, Tracy Chapman and others, not only lent their support, but also put their prestige on the line when they asked the Grandmothers and the Mothers of the Plaza de Mayo to come on the stage.

On this occasion, these artists, together with the Mothers and Grandmothers, did something that the public supported and embraced with an incredible sense of responsibility and great emotion. It was an audience which had gathered especially for their generation's music, but which was receptive to Amnesty's message: it became the evening's protagonist. Just imagine tens of thousands of small lights blinking like a palpitating heart accompanying the songs, accompanying our cause in the darkness.

For us Mothers, who were determined to go up on the stage without much thought about how well or badly we played our parts, it meant that finally we would have access to the TV screens in every home in Argentina. It was the only opportunity that we mothers had for appearing on Argentinian television even under a democratic government. Such an international event was necessary for this to happen. During all of our struggle, the Argentinian media had never given us any significant time or space.

In time we were able to appreciate the value that the Amnesty Concert had for human rights. At first this new form of broadcasting disconcerted and astonished us because it was so completely different from our concept of the struggle. But it turned out to be a magnificent vehicle of communication.

We were never given any preferential treatment by the media, especially by the television industry in Argentina, so that we were forced to make our cause known in every imaginable way, but had never reached the masses, as we did on this occasion.

We Mothers organized talks, round tables, photograph exhibits, art festivals with the participation of popular artists, and showed the movie called "The Mothers of the Plaza de Mayo," directed by Lupe Portillo and Susana Muñoz.

We showed it at the Centro Cultural San Martín, at neighborhood cultural centers, schools, student centers and sometimes in plazas and public parks. One of the last showings took place at the 1989 Book Fair, where passersby stopped and finally stayed to watch, sitting on the floor until it ended. We have always tried to make the most of the visible cracks in the constitutional government, which was forever worried that we might have too much exposure. Still, we remain convinced that all this work serves to make sure that our people don't forget the disappearances.

A PROPOSAL FOR THE UNITED NATIONS

More than three hundred leaders of human rights organizations and of jurists from Latin America, Europe and the United States supported, by acclamation, the proposal presented at the colloquium held at the School of Law and Social Sciences of the University of Buenos Aires between October 10 and 13, 1988.

We Mothers were invited to attend this colloquium on the way the Law was addressing the problem of the forced disappearances.

In spite of the blows sustained in the field of legislation, the shadow of the disappeared continued to bear witness and it was precisely in Buenos Aires that this important meeting was organized. Thirty-two national and international organizations participated, among them the National Council of Churches, WOLA, SOLMA (Solidarity with the Mothers), the Swiss Committee against Torture, the New York Lawyers' Association, Amnesty International, Americas Watch, the Vicariate of Solidarity from Chile and the Ecumenical Movement for Human Rights.

The fundamental objective of this colloquium was to bring before the United Nations a proposal to make the forced disappearance of persons a "crime of lèse humanité."

We mothers stress how important it is to make the crime of forced disappearance punishable. That is why the accomplishment of this colloquium moved us deeply.

The proposal also demands that all courts bring the perpetrators to judgment where they are found, and prohibits all subscriber countries from granting them political asylum.

There were words of encouragement and praise for the Mothers' struggle in almost all the speeches. And moments of emotion and pleasant informal exchanges were not lacking.

When we were going to the conference room before the start of one of the sessions, I saw a young man surrounded by children who were playing with him and trying to stop him from lighting a cigarette. The affectionate exchanges between Judge Juan Ramos Padilla and the grandchildren recovered by the Grandmothers of the Plaza de Mayo gave me great pleasure. I stayed and observed them for a while.

I felt intense emotion watching these children running and playing when I reflected that they had been in the hands of people who were not members of their families and that they had been handed over by oppressors and outsiders. These children had been born in jail or they had been separated from their parents upon their abduction. And now they were here and so happy. It seemed like a miracle.

Judge Padilla had the pleasure of being able to return so many children to their legitimate families.

Beyond the emotional moment experienced with those recovered children, this episode showed that every struggle will at last bring compensation for the great effort made, and it also created an optimistic setting for the ideas inspired by the colloquium.

THE MOTHERS OF THE PLAZA DE MAYO—THE FOUNDING GROUP

After so many years of anguish and muzzling by censorship, when at last we had the possibility of giving loud voice to our silent screams and our demands and hopes for a prompt answer, irreconcilable differences painfully split our movement. First we tried to start a parallel group but unfortunately we were forced to start the new association to which I belong: Mothers of the Plaza de Mayo—Founding Group.

One of the main differences that started to divide us was our differing stances regarding the democratic government. Some of the Mothers maintained that there was no difference between the military dictatorship and the government chosen by the people: they were not giving us any answers. But our group saw a fundamental difference: the constitutional government betrayed the cause of the disappeared, but notwithstanding we have been able to broadcast the subject of human rights to a degree impossible during the dictatorship. Books have been printed, movies have been produced, magazines have been published, student centers have reappeared, some children of the disappeared have been recovered, the subject of the repression has begun to be the theme of debates and of congresses....

Another fundamental disagreement was around the exhumation of bodies. The Founding Group maintains that the decision to recover the remains of disappeared family members in those cases in which they are scientifically identified is very personal. Moreover, the Group acts as a guarantor for the young anthropologists who devote themselves to this work, and it accompanies each family at the moment of the exhumation and recovery of the remains of their loved ones. We consider this to be an imperative human need, one deeply rooted in culture and religion. But the group that Hebe de Bonafini leads absolutely rejects these exhumations.

We find ourselves separated from our sisters, but we never confront each other; we all persevere in our firm decision not to give up.

TESTIMONIES

I look at you who look at me,
who perhaps would like to know,
and I, from my tremendous clarity,
I, from my insomnia,
am going to ask you,
if you have any children...

ILDA IRRUSTITA DE MICUCCI
mother of
VIVIANA MICUCCI
abducted at 25 years of age and
DANIEL MICUCCI
abducted at 22 years of age
on November 11, 1976

I am glad that we are talking today, because yesterday I had an experience that touched me and made me cry as I haven't cried in a long time. But I am glad to be able to cry because sometimes I fear I am becoming hardened. It really scares me. You know, I often think about it.

My two children, Viviana, 25 years old and Daniel, 22 years old, were taken—together—on November 11, 1976.

The operation took place very early in the morning. A lot of men arrived at our house looking for Daniel. Daniel had already left for the company he worked for in Pilar. And they took Viviana and said that they were only going to interrogate her and that we would hear about her on the following day. After they left, my husband and I didn't know what to do. The only thing we could think of was to get in the car and go to Pilar to let Daniel know what had happened. When we arrived, the operatives were already there, some of them the same ones who had been at our house, plus other new ones. They detained us and they took all three of us: Daniel, Pepe and myself in separate cars. They put hoods on us during the ride and we went to an area we didn't know and which we couldn't see because of the hoods. There Pepe and I were kept, hooded and handcuffed all the time, until the following night. They did not interrogate us at any time, but we didn't see our children either, either of them, nor did we hear anything about them. On the following day, at night, they freed us

182

near the Pan-American Highway. They left us on a very dark road, and from there we returned home and began our struggle to find out what had happened to our children.

Without any news

We exhausted all the resources we had; Pepe was the first to start moving, inquiring. I would stay home, waiting for a call, anything that would bring us news. Pepe started the inquiries first with the people he knew in the Navy, the Army, the prefecture. But they would tell him in one branch of the armed forces that they didn't know what the other branches were doing. When we had exhausted all the legal processes, the habeas corpuses, and all the visits to people that we thought had some influence, we realized that there was no answer.

That was when I started to despair. Then I thought that if only all the parents who were in similar circumstances would join forces and do things together, we would get some concrete news.

I go to the Plaza

One day Pepe called me from his office. He had retired from the Prefecture years before, and presently he had an agency on Diagonal Norte and Florida Street. On that day he had seen a group of people at the Plaza de Mayo. I don't know why he thought that they had something in common with us. When he got off the bus he approached them, but for the first moments he felt rejected because they were all women and if a man approached, they acted suspicious. And he realized it. Well, this is how he learnt about the existence of these people who were the initial group of the

Mothers. This must have been more or less around August 1977, at the time Cyrus Vance arrived.

Pepe told me to leave everything and to go there immediately, because a group of women who were at the Plaza were going to meet that afternoon and go to the offices of the *Buenos Aires Herald*, so that I should go to see those people. Thus I arrived at the Plaza and went to the *Buenos Aires Herald* with this group of women. I didn't know anybody. I had just met them. At the *Buenos Aires Herald*, Cox's secretary received us because Cox was not there at the moment; nevertheless, each of the women told her story, gave her testimony. And it was then that I really began to hear many parallel stories, and about so many similar circumstances.

And it was then that I began to act together with the Mothers, and we embarked upon anything that we thought would be useful, or that we imagined could be useful.

I want to point out that the fact that Pepe had belonged to the armed forces didn't help us at all. There were people who really did try to help us, but soon I realized that they were people who really didn't have any idea of the magnitude of the situation. And when they did try to find out something to help us, only then did they become conscious of what was going on and of what was really happening. Because even though they belonged to the armed forces, I think there were people engaged in other activities who were ignorant of what was really going on.

Another point that I want to stress is that for Pepe, all this was overwhelming. His career had been something very important in his life, he was very proud of belonging to the armed forces, to the Prefecture above all. And suddenly he found himself in a situation like this and, found society rejecting everything that the military institutions represented.

There were still parts of society that were not yet conscious of what was going on—but to feel the rejection of the community we had established ties with was at that moment so very painful! Because we had to establish relationships, and to work, and to fight together with all the families who were affected. Soon we were surrounded by people who when talking about the armed forces used a tone full of hatred, hatred that I also came to feel and which I tried to hide from my husband. I could not pretend very well and that affected him because he found himself divided. He really became divided into two parts, one part the father who lost his children and who had to do the impossible to recover them, and the other part formed by his military background.

I believe that this was one of the things that hurt the most. You know, he died without having gotten any news about his children. Actually, we never got any news. But nevertheless, I remained eager to fight in whatever way I could and with what I could, to do whatever was feasible, because I could not imagine then (or even now) that they would never reappear. And like all the Mothers, I keep on demanding an explanation about what has been done with our children.

My children

My children were two excellent kids, good students, hard workers, both of them. Daniel had graduated as a chemical technician at the Otto Krause Institute. The same year he graduated and during his first vacation, he took a course to enter the University, and that same year he started his military service as a volunteer at the Prefecture, precisely so that once he started his university career, he wouldn't have to interrupt it. As soon as he finished his military service, on his own he got a job as a chemical technician at Argentine Aniline (a chemical used in dyes, medicines, and explosives). At the same time he continued with his studies, so that he went from his job to school. When the company opened a plant in Pilar, they offered him a position there as the head of the plant. He was then 22 years old and was the head of the plant at Pilar. He was very sensitive, introverted, didn't show much, didn't talk much, he was a kid of few words, but he knew how to be supportive during difficult moments. Viviana was very different. She was extroverted, very much into talking about all her concerns, very cheerful, full of ideas about how to deal with things. During the family's birthday parties, she always showed her sense of humor. She was very warm, very interested in everything, wanted to learn everything, took courses in thousands of things. It seemed as if she wanted to absorb everything that happened around her. She graduated as a teacher and then entered Philosophy and Letters so as to go on to study Library Sciences. When she began her university studies, she started to work at a public library in Martinez. After that she had a substitute position as a librarian at the San Isidro National College and then, following up a newspaper ad, she began to work as a librarian at the Zoonosis Pan-American Center, which was located on one of the floors of Posadas Hospital, and which is affiliated with the World Health Organization.

So that her life was a very, very intense one of work and study.

At that time, we had a little dog, Pelusa. I knew when the children came home because Pelusa would move her little ears, get up, and run to the door. As soon as the bus that brought them stopped, she knew that the kids were returning. After my children's disappearances, and when our hopes had started vanishing, I observed my little dog again. At the beginning, she would become agitated when the usual time of their return came near, but then...I would look at her anxiously, waiting for some sign, since they were saying that the children were still alive and perhaps they would be freed at any time. But, unluckily, Pelusa stopped moving around and showing any signs of recognition. I would watch her, but she was impassive. She didn't show any nervousness or expectation ever again, as if she knew that they would never return. She knew it before I did.

SARA SILVER DE BRODSKY
mother of
FERNANDO RUBEN BRODSKY
abducted at the age of 22 on August 14, 1979

I remember Fernando very well when he was quite young, when he did the painting which I see from where I am sitting. In that painting, Fernando is like the center in the midst of an amusement park. At this moment—and for some time—I have not known what's going on. I remember him physically, but I can't talk much about him and this painting allows me to see how he was the center because of his way of being, because of his youth, because of his poetic feeling for life, because of what we had taught him: that art in man can overcome much human evil.

I see him like a lantern surrounded by all this that appears to be color, shape...a possible discovery of the world that he would have liked to have had. I see him inside the painting and, truly, I don't see him, because he has disappeared.

I would like to replace him

Fernando was a boy who already had his personality formed when he was thirteen years old. Every time I think

187

about him, I love him more. I say this because of his very sober, introverted way of being. He was dark-skinned, dark and thin—he was already a man, practically. He was restless, he was starting to be moved by the many needs of his own development. And when he was twenty-two years old, when they took him away, he was already a tall, strong kid.

My son was in Brazil for a year and a half. We didn't want him to come back. He left in 1977. We got him out of the country because he was helping marginal people, and that was not looked upon with favorable eyes here.

He did things that I would like to do today. What I would love to do today with my life is to replace him. Because he was a psychology student, he was working with Alcoholics Anonymous in workers' neighborhoods. The work he had chosen was a long-term proposition. But since he was studying, he would surely put knowledge and practice together later on. Fernando was twenty-two years old. I could describe to you how those individuals—horrible as they are for me—I mean from the armed forces, took him away...no other group of individuals could have the power they have.

Fernando was in Brazil and my other children weren't here either, because, well, many of the students from the Buenos Aires National had already disappeared. My older son, Marcelo, attended this same high school. And Fernando, after living in Brazil for a year and a half, returned. He knew his father and I were living alone in Buenos Aires, so he didn't want to be far away. We had missed him enormously. He came back and stayed with a friend from the National School. But he was always with us. We used to go sailing, to the movies.... He also had his own activities. He had gotten a job at a school. He was teaching drama and he had a passion for his students. What I remember is that he was in Buenos Aires and that something happened to him that made him even more introverted. I mean that it was even more difficult to communicate with him. And even

188

when we kept on asking him the reason for his return, the only thing he would say is that he wanted to be here, and especially to be with his family. What happened is that he was also studying at the University. He became more and more active in Buenos Aires, and even when we kept telling him: "Look Fernando, this is no place to be, because very serious things keep on happening here," he insisted on staying. And so I believed that the horror of the disappearances and deaths were over; I lived a little more at ease, because my son was coming and going and I was seeing him often. I couldn't imagine that those people, after fighting against the "guerrillas," and after killing or disappearing I don't know how many people, could keep on doing the same thing. Nevertheless, they took him too. We learnt that men from the Navy were waiting for him at his house since seven in the evening on August 14, 1979. Fernando arrived from the University that evening at around eleven-thirty. When he went into the bathroom, one of the them was waiting for him. They took him away, forcing him with a rifle into a white Ford.

He was so generous, the very best of human beings. And this Argentinian military, under the pretext of a Western and Christian lifestyle, committed the most serious abuses. They stole him from me. I went all over the world searching for him. And I cannot picture my son in this way: "disappeared."

The disappearance

"Disappearance" was the term used by the people in that government. I was part of this country and believed that what had happened to thousands of mothers wouldn't happen to me. But just the same, when I called the school on the phone, they told me he had not come to teach (he hadn't gone to see his grandfather either on Tuesday, when

189

he was supposed to have lunch with him). It is true that he had had dinner with us on the previous day. It was a very special dinner because our friend Quino and his wife, Alicia, came. And that was on the day before they took him away. That night Fernando stayed to sleep. He was very happy because of what we had shared. On the following day he said goodbye. He was going to school. Evidently, later on he went to the university and when he got back to his place, they detained him.

I am still paralyzed by a force inside me that is born of fear, anger, and hatred. I had to find my son, I didn't have any doubts about that. I was going to find him because Fernando was at his place when they came to take him. Besides, his neighbors were witnesses. A whole battalion came for my son, Fernando Rubén Brodsky. My son must have been very important to these people, for them to want him disappeared. I began to search for him. On that day, August 14th, on the 15th or 16th I looked for him at the school. He wasn't there, not at work, not at his place. I went directly to the human rights organizations. But since in Buenos Aires at this time, the families were mobilizing because the OAS was coming to see what was going on in the city regarding human rights, I presented myself to them. During those days, we were lining up to complain about the disappearances. And that is when the trucks passed by filled with young people madly screaming because we had won a soccer championship! And that was the time of the famous official slogan: "We Argentinians are upright and humane."

Governor Colombo received my husband and offered him the possibility of seeing Harguindeguy in Buenos Aires. When my husband got back, I had already gone to find out where Fernando's closest friend was—Pablo Lepiscopo.

Since my husband is an eye doctor and treats many people, he had also treated the father of a former girlfriend of Fernando. So I go to this girl's house before going to the OAS. I want to find out if she knows where Pablo Lepiscopo is. I talk to Bettina, who had been my son's girlfriend, and she tells me that they had detained her for twenty-four hours. Then I find out that Pablo had also been detained. Bettina tells me that she thinks Fernando was detained too.

My husband makes inquiries by himself, because I am like a madwoman, I can't believe they have snatched my son from me. My husband goes to the presidential palace and sees Harguindeguy, and Harguindeguy tells him to see somebody else, Ruiz Palacio. These are people who look at you as if from a height, and you ask yourself: "Who am I down here?" And I also ask myself: "Who are they up there?" They have a way of speaking as if they were the innocent ones and we were the guilty. Evidently, there are two realities: theirs—they know what they are handing out, lies—and ours: we have come to put in our demand for our son's life in a state of innocence and ingenuousness. After that interview, my husband came home very depressed and sick. Desperate, I tell him: "Dear, we can't give up, we have to keep on looking, they have to return Fernando to me," and my husband answers: "Yes, but how?" "I don't know, we have to talk to somebody, somebody who can provide us with some information." And he tells me: "Look, at this moment I have Dr. Robledo as a patient. He must be in the know." Then we talk to him and he gets us an interview with Massera. We go, and the person who receives us intimates that we are in good hands. Then Massera sees us in person and tells us to come back in one or two weeks. When we return, I bring him a small sculpture by Antonio Pujia representing God's hand as a sign of appreciation for having received us. His son greets us and is a bit surprised by the gift.

After that we meet with an officer who shows signs of knowing Fernando.

My son and his grandfather

Then we start to realize that Fernando is at the Navy Mechanics' School.

Every Saturday and Sunday I go by the School because we suspected it was there that my son was.

Only when CONADEP was created did we know it for sure, because there are six or seven people who saw him and were with him in that concentration camp.

My son was kept between two very close wooden partitions. They didn't allow me to see him. I was not able to see him.

I couldn't accept the fact that my son was inside the Mechanics' School—and that is my emotional problem, my impotence, my frustration, my insecurity.

We started criminal charges against the Armed Forces at the San Isidro Court House: case number 8893, which is still open, because we learnt that my son was there at the Mechanics' School, whose commanding officer was Lambruschini. In the midst of this chaotic situation of searching for my son, I needed a clear head to confront and denounce the enemy, although I myself felt as if I were in a huge concentration camp.

I want to tell about the relationship between Fernando and his grandfather.

He was very affectionate with him. They met on Thursdays to play chess. Fernando always carried a gold medal that his grandfather had given him. He had won it at fifteen in a chess championship. Fernando had it with him when he was abducted. When Fernando called on the phone from his place of imprisonment—he must have called me from there about fifteen times—during one of these calls, I asked him about his grandfather's medal, and he told me that surely they would return it when they freed him. How could I have thought that those people who had my son would not free him? I ask myself now, where do these monsters, these accomplices in the deaths of human beings go? Our children are our civilization's heroes, they were young people worthy of being Argentinians, beautiful, loved, in a world I am sorry we have to live in. We Mothers form a chain of people who are also always searching for dignity and for the truth, and who want to know why all this happened in our country, Argentina.

Yesterday, October 28, 1986, I was walking on the street and crying. Seven years have gone by since my adored son's disappearance.

But Fernando has left me this message: that I should replace him in his task, his work. His message was: "Mother, keep on defending people who don't have the means to help themselves; help them."

ALICIA RIVAROLA DE CÁRDENAS
mother of
ALVARO CÁRDENAS
abducted at 23 years of age, on November 9, 1976

It took time for me to be able to talk about my son

My son disappeared on November 9, 1976.

Many months went by until I was able to talk about my detained-disappeared son. I had a psychological problem, as if it were a taboo. I couldn't speak his name. That does not mean I was not going everywhere to protest. I went first to the Permanent Assembly, then to the League of Human Rights. I found a group of families there, and I joined them, but I could not mention my son's name.... It was really odd. I started going to a psychologist who helped me a great deal. I went to see her for some time, then she found me better, but then—ah!...after going to the Families' group, I was told about Thursdays and the Mothers of the Plaza de Mayo. I started going to the Plaza de Mayo, and being around so many fellow beings with the same problem, the inhibition disappeared. I started to talk about the abduction, about what happened, what my son was like....

What had happened to me before—when I wanted to talk about my son—it seemed as if I couldn't bring the words out, the anguish was so great that it left me speechless. Now I understand what was the matter with me: the desperation and the anguish didn't allow me to voice judgment and words about the operation that took place at home, about my son's detention and his disappearance....

If I was able to overcome it, it was because I joined the Mothers, because I started going to the Plaza, and because I began to direct all that anguish into the struggle.

I also realize now that it is good for me to talk about my son's personality, his ideals, about how he started to feel the need to fight against injustice when he was in high school. It was then that I understood my son's sense of social justice. My husband and I would always comment: "While other boys his age devote Sundays to having fun, he busies himself with abandoned children who don't have either the opportunity or access to places of amusement."

Really, his attitude surprised both of us. One of the things he was always criticizing was the fact that in our country there still could be people performing domestic service. He could not understand it.

My son went to a religious school. We liked that because we saw that this school was not class conscious. And because our boy was happy going to school, he fit in well. Even outside his hours of study, he used to meet other fellow students at the Student Center. He had a happy, full life.

He was a very good fellow student and friend, and the others reciprocated. For all these years they have shown their solidarity, accompanying us in the marches...they never forget his birthday....

I remember him as happy, with a great sense of humor, very affectionate, loving, concerned about his family.

He fell in love with a girl who shared the same concerns and ideas. And two days before the abduction, he had invited us to meet her mother. It seems that on the previous day they had been together and they had been followed. This girl was murdered, and we found out later that they delivered her remains to her family. During that time, the newspapers were always publishing news of episodes with the police or military which were later proved nonexistent. Just in the same way that the citizens were being lied to, they made us suffer with our treks to the Ministry of the Interior. Every month they tried to give us the illusion that we would be able to get some news, knowing full well that this was false. I believe this was one of the most cruel and sadistic aspects of those years of dictatorship. They had us—all the relatives of the detained-disappeared—coming to the Ministry of the Interior once a month.

We held on to hope

They kept on torturing us for eight years at least with that illusion. And naively, we kept holding on to hope, knowing deep down that they would never tell us anything. But if we lost that hope, we would lose everything.

In general, I didn't have the support of my friends, including my long-term friends, who didn't understand our tragedy and who didn't take our side. I felt comfortable with the Mothers, who had suffered what I had. Frankly, I suffered tremendous disappointments from people, friends from whom I had to keep distant because they kept talking about a war that never took place. They defended the "process."

I haven't yet mentioned my son's name. His name is Alvaro Cárdenas. He was twenty-three years old when they carried him off. The operation was manned by some fourteen people dressed in fatigues and carrying rifles. They took us out to the sidewalk around 3:00 in the morning, and they stayed inside with my son, questioning him for about an hour. Then they took him away. We could not see him because they had us against the wall under orders not to utter a word.

When we got back into the house, we found everything strewn all over, pictures on the floor, the closets emptied— great disorder.

There was a change in the whole family because of Alvaro's abduction. Even our personalities were altered. I have always been a very quiet person. Now, sometimes I am aggressive, I answer people's questions in a bad mood. I believe that every family that has suffered from a similar tragedy cannot recover, cannot be the way they were.

My younger son—eight years younger than Alvaro— suffered from an emotional shock because of what took place. He stopped studying. He didn't want to do anything. He would go to school, go in one door and out the other. It took him about five years to recover, thanks to a very good therapist. Once recovered, he did his secondary education at an evening school. Then he entered the School of Dramatic Arts and graduated as an actor. He has a normal life, but the wound is still there. The horrible image of the abduction is there.

I realize that all the affected families are not alike. The harm that has been inflicted is very great, not only to us, but to the whole society. It is different when a mother loses her child because of some sickness or some accident. She can bury him, take him flowers. We don't know how they died, not even if they did die.

That is how they interrupted our lives, our families' lives, and they also interrupted our country's history.

I am never going to give up our struggle in search of the truth and of justice. Though Alvaro may be disappeared, I always feel his presence near me and the proof of that is the group of his friends: they often meet. I am sure he is present with them.

CHAPTER 7

THE MOTHERS TODAY

Alone

You are alone/ earth/ of the compañeros
whom you now enfold and decompose/
you hear them as they let go slowly
of the love that remains to them/ let slip
their time of falling/ dream their dreams/ quiet/
never again to see those faces which hold them/
they loom up/ continued/ in this sun/
that was once the sun of justice

Juan Gelman
translated by Joan Lindgren

Note: Marcelo Gelman was exhumed in 1989. The wake
took place at the UTPBA (Press-Workers Union of
Buenos Aires) and he was buried on January 6, 1990.
[MM]

WHY DO WE CONTINUE THE CIRCLE?

The Mothers' circle still goes on. We are maintaining the vigil, sleepless, awake, day and night. We are urged on because we don't want to lose everything we have gained and because we want to reach our goal.

To maintain a vigil is not just the sacrifice of physical sleep; a vigil also allows us to exercise our capacity to reason and use our thought processes. This is what vigil means to us. We continue to go to the Plaza in order to keep alive the fire we lit on the first day.

Nowadays, people from all over the world visit us, people who have found out that we won't give up and who humbly wish to show us their support. Artists, newspapermen, politicians, sociologists. They invariably ask us: "But, what do you expect now? Why do you keep on going to the Plaza?" And we always answer: "They have given us no answers, in spite of all our marching, all our efforts and despair. The circle continues because the injustice continues."

They tried to satisfy us by forming CONADEP and with the trials of the members of the junta. They gave us a sample of all the horror that took place. But it did not take long for them to back off. Agreements with groups in power and pressure from the military crushed a legitimate solution. And for it they want to substitute reconciliation by decree.

Because of all this and because we have resisted their treason, we will hold on for as long as necessary to see justice done.

This circle, which began so timidly, has become wider in its objectives; in addition to our search, it now represents the wish to spread our own moral consciousness in the cause of human rights.

We Mothers of the Plaza de Mayo constitute one of the first movements of resistance organized against forced disappearances, even though that despicable practice had already started in other Latin American countries like Guatemala, Chile, and El Salvador. And our circle generated organized protest movements in other American countries. Starting in the '80s we saw other women just like us in other countries protesting and carrying the photographs of their loved ones.

Our vigil encourages the struggle for human rights.

BECAUSE LIFE IS SACRED

I find in the words of Albert Einstein (a thinker who brilliantly described the meaning of life) everything that we so laboriously try to express in so many thousands of ways: "Each person's life has meaning only if it is in the service of beautifying and ennobling everything that exists. Life is sacred; this means that it is the supreme value from which everything else emanates. The sanctification of the life that embraces more than oneself carries with it the supreme value of everything spiritual."

Without any exceptions, each of us has become very conscious of this, so that for this reason we can no longer abandon the circle. Carmen Cobo and María Adela have expressed the notion as part of their statement in these words which I have taken from their testimony:

WITH A CLEAN FACE

"Our children were not taken as prisoners from a battlefield; totally defenseless, they were abducted from their homes, from the street, from their places of study and work. After their abduction they were tortured, violated; many of them were murdered, and babies, children, adolescents, young people and old people were taken. Our struggle has taken years of ceaseless searching and every other possible method, but it has been carried out by legal, constitutional, non-violent methods—with a clean face." (Carmen Cobo).

"We want to vindicate our children, their ideas, their dreams, their yearnings, their purposes by telling about what they were, not only what they wanted. We Mothers, whether we realize it or not, have accepted our children's struggle. We want to know from whom the orders came and who carried them out, and how our children were vilely murdered: who killed them and where their bodies are, whether thrown in the sea, buried, or incinerated. In every place where a human being was tortured, violated, and humiliated in every possible way, we want a sign to be placed, a plaque, a marker that says: 'Here the most contemptible forms of torture were used and it must not happen ever again. Never again.'" (María Adela).

BECAUSE THERE ARE NINETY THOUSAND OF THE DISAPPEARED IN LATIN AMERICA

Regrettably, this long, sad Argentinian night was not exclusive to our country. We now know of ninety thousand disappeared all over Latin America.

We have Ida Tatter's testimony about this drama. Ida Tatter is a Paraguayan companion in the struggle, who joined the Mothers and constantly protested for her husband's life and for the many Paraguayans disappeared in Argentina.

IDALINA RÁDICE DE TATTER'S TESTIMONY

My husband's name is Federico Jorge Tatter, a Paraguayan of German descent who was extremely worried about the problems in our country, where we have had a dictatorial regime for over forty years. Exiled in Argentina, we were again subjected to repression; my husband disappeared after the 1976 coup, my younger son had to leave for Mexico and my two other sons also had to leave Paraguay for exile; consequently, my family has been dispersed. Although my husband had been detained many times in Paraguay, and even tortured, I don't know how to characterize his detention-disappearance. It has been something truly monstrous.

My husband disappeared on October 23, 1976 when he was 56 years old. My reaction was swift and wide-reaching. I went to Command One and have gone there as many as five times a day; I believe I have topped the record for "habeas corpuses," I have covered the embassies, all the churches, consulted with almost every bishop. I have devoted myself to nothing but searching for him, and have always been given the same answer: they don't know anything.

Although the dictatorship planned for the disappearances, it didn't foresee our reaction. We started meeting with our companions, we began to meet to talk about what had happened to us.

Something I would like to remember—among the very many things we have done together during these years—is the campaign to gather signatures we carried out with several other organizations in 1982. Its purpose was to make a presentation of signatures, not only those of family

203

members, but also of people from the community who through their signing seemed to be accompanying us in person. The objective was also to explain what was going on in Argentina; nobody signed before receiving a full explanation of the problem of the disappearance of people. And though it was difficult to achieve, within the equivalent of four city blocks sixty percent signed, for there were many people who already knew through a relative or a friend that there were individuals who had disappeared.

We have also organized the families of disappeared Paraguayans who, as in my case, have come to Argentina for political reasons. There are around sixty disappeared and our objective is clear: to show that a double repression took place; we were subjected to repression in our country and here in Argentina as well.

BECAUSE THERE ARE STILL CASES OF DISAPPEARED CHILDREN

There are Mothers who are also Grandmothers. And all of us want to recover those grandchildren, our children's children. To recover the identities of those children and return them to their legitimate families is a concrete part of the struggle. This is another answer to the question: why does the circle continue?

With their tenacity and courage the Grandmothers have recovered twenty-five children, and there are still many more whom we need to recover.

It is essential for me to add the testimony of María Isabel de Mariani (president of the Grandmothers of the Plaza de Mayo) to this unique report, one we all shared in common.

We imagine that every disappeared woman who knew she was pregnant or who had other children, would have fervently desired them to recover their freedom and be reunited with their legitimate family.

THE TESTIMONY OF
MARIA ISABEL CHOROBIK DE MARIANI

I had been looking for my little granddaughter since November, 1976—alone, like all the Mothers who have been looking for loved ones—without knowing where to go. I personally went to the courts, army posts, police stations, and neighborhoods, without knowing that there were more disappeared, without knowing the meaning of the word disappeared, believing that I didn't know how to find my granddaughter, never imagining that she could have ever been a victim of an abduction or a disappearance. I waited for telephone calls that never came, for a bell to ring every night which would bring my little girl back to me.

In the midst of my many searches somebody asked me if I had been to a juvenile court. I knew what that was but I was ignorant of the kind of minors they dealt with. I assumed these minors were those described as "delinquents" or abandoned street children. So I found out where there was a juvenile court and one day I went there. I was lucky to find Dr. Lydia Pegenaute, who to my great surprise, received me very well. She told me that I was not the first woman to have come with my problem, that there were two other women who were looking for their little grandchildren who had been born in captivity. At that time the words "in prison" were used because we assumed that after having disappeared, people were kept as prisoners. This lady told me: "Señora, how alone you are!" But I thought that by saying this she was referring to my personal situation: my husband was in Europe and I no longer had my father.

I felt her support very strongly; she took risks searching for my granddaughter, she made all the inquiries she could and all those that I proposed. And one day she repeated again: "Señora, you are so alone!" And then I understood that if I searched together with other grandmothers, more doors would open up. Timidly I asked her for the name of the other women she knew. She quickly gave them to me and so I made connections with Alicia Shobasnabar de la Cuadra, who also lived in La Plata. All this happened in La Plata. At her house I found out that there was another group of women—mothers—who were searching together for their children, and some also for their grandchildren, who by that date must have already been born. I also learnt that a group of mothers met at the Plaza de Mayo, that they gave petitions to the National Government, something I had not thought of doing. All my inquiries had been made in La Plata.

On that day, we talked a lot and Alicia ("Bicha" to us) told me that Mr. Cyrus Vance, a very important North American, was about to arrive, and that each of the Mothers would hand him a petition, together with a testimony describing her case. She asked me to come; I went, very apprehensively, of course. I believe that we were all afraid at the beginning. When I arrived at the Plaza San Martín I encountered policemen who looked at us with their hyena faces and with their machine guns trained at us. There I met other grandmothers and mothers; I will always remember their faces at that moment. I was expecting to find people with the same kind of expression I had—or that I thought I had—one which showed all the pain through which we were living. But instead they were smiling at me. I thought it magnificent that those women were smiling despite of the fact that we were living the same pain. For me, it was a jolt of strength which kept me going. I also carried my prepared testimony to give to Cyrus Vance. It was October, 1977. People ran, crowding together; the women shouted, asking for help for their children. And I did too, without knowing what to do, paper in hand. At that moment, a woman approached and asked me: "Did you hand in your paper?" "No," I told her. I held it tight in my hand. The important person was leaving and the men in uniform at the Plaza were ordering us to go away. "Give it to me, give it to me!" she shouted. She took the paper and ran. Getting into the midst of the security forces, she went through the line of armed policemen, followed Mr. Vance and handed him the testimony on my granddaughter and her parents, and came back. Afterwards, I learnt that this woman was Azucena Villaflor, the Mother who disappeared on December of the same year.

Right there, under an ombú tree I sat for a while with the grandmothers I had just met. I found out that some of them were attending meetings of the League of Human Rights, others of the Permanent Assembly, asking them for help. But all of them were participating in the Plaza de Mayo circle, and some belonged to the Mothers of the Plaza de Mayo. I also started going to the Thursday circles.

On the way home, we kept on talking about an idea Alicia and I had come with, how all the grandmothers could get together and do the search in unison. And so we decided to do this. From that moment until today, we stay together, asking for justice. We decided to make a list of the newly-born babies or those about to be born; the only one we knew about at this time was Clara Anahí, my granddaughter, the rest were babies still to be born, since their mothers were pregnant when they were abducted. We also made a list of the judges at the juvenile courts. We could not think of another place where we could make inquiries, and we started to go around in weekly groups of three to each juvenile court asking for information and requesting to be informed about any "No Name" children coming under the jurisdiction of the court so that they could be given to us for adoption—since they could be our grandchildren. At the same time, we were searching for our children. The Grandmothers of the Plaza de Mayo organization was specifically devoted to the search for disappeared children. Our methods are a little bit different from those of the Mothers. The paths used are of another sort since the children were separated from their parents; we intuitively knew this from the start. We originally thought they were in the hands of the abductors.

207

Since 1976, we have requested that those children be given to us for adoption.

I want to make it clear that unfortunately the judicial procedure for each case—even in the most recent cases—does not explain what has happened to the parents even when the children are found.

At the beginning, we formed a group without pretending to organize new human rights activities: we were a group of women who made requests together before the courts of justice. We were simply looking for our grandchildren and our children from morning to night, without respite.

We also appealed to the Church, which denied us any information about the children as well as the grandchildren.

You ask me what I did it to fill up my life after so much despair and loneliness. I have trouble talking about myself. I have practically forgotten all about that. It so happens that we Grandmothers have only one subject: our grandchildren. What can I tell you? That, for instance, I very much like reading and doing things with my hands: ceramics and knitting? I had to abandon certain things for lack of time.

In the case of knitting, I became traumatized: on the day they machine-gunned my son's house, I was knitting a little garment for my granddaughter. I could not go back to it and that work remains unfinished. Many years have gone by and I never again took up knitting until last year. Estela Carlotto, the Grandmothers' vice president, and I were in Geneva at the United Nations at a time when the Argentinian delegation challenged us about a report made by Professor Theo Van Boven concerning children taken captive in Paraguay. Estela and I felt terrible. The following day we woke up in anguish—we didn't feel like doing a thing. We stayed in our room in the hotel thinking about a way to face this new reversal and how to forge ahead. We both looked at each other at the same time and said: "Shall we buy some yarn?" It was years since either of us had knitted. We went out to buy yarn and needles and we sat on the bed, silent, and started to

208

knit. Hours went by. Finally we laughed and said: "How wonderful! We have gotten rid of our anguish by knitting."

So many things have given us the strength to continue with our struggle! So many shows of solidarity and affection! We were once in Holland at a clergyman's house. We were telling him our tribulations without noticing the presence of a five year old little girl. Of course, she didn't understand our language, but she sensed something and she questioned her mother. To our great surprise she brought us a drawing she'd done while we were talking. And she asked us if the children that we Grandmothers were looking for were like them. We were moved to tears and then, by agreement with all the Grandmothers, we decided that the image in the picture was going to be our symbol. Going back to the subject of the grandchildren, what shall we say about the recovered children?

We can't stop talking when we speak about them. They are so well! Sometimes it astonishes us that with all they have suffered they could be in such good condition. But we have concluded that they are very strong kids. If they were able to survive the conditions of their birth in captivity, and as babies, of being wrenched from their families, it means that they knew how to defend themselves. Just as in Paulita's case, who defended her name when the kidnappers tried to change it, calling her Luisa. She was hardly two years old, but when they would call her Luisa, she'd say: "No, Paula," so Paula it remained and she is Paula.

Our children grow fast, they develop emotionally, they knit themselves into their legitimate families in a natural way, and this is due to the fact that they have had to hide their feelings. There are expressions that have come from these children, used with people they know and whom they have become fond of, like the girl who says: "I was like in a closed room and suddenly the door opened and I came out"; another says: "I wasn't growing up because it seemed like I had a hand on top of my head. They removed the hand when they returned me, and I grew": things like that, in their own language, expressing themselves in their own way, so they return to life; before, they were hibernating.

Each grandchild was placed in different circumstances: for instance, a little boy who had been carried away when his parents were abducted and left at a juvenile court, was recovered almost miraculously. One of the court's employees, who was especially fond of the boy, would take him to her house to sleep and every morning would take him back to the court house and wait for him to be placed. On one of those nights, he saw an actress on the TV screen and called very excitedly: "Auntie! Auntie!" Actually, the child's aunt was a well-known actress. The woman who was caring for him understood that she was close to finding his family and let the judge know it. That little one, just three years old, is one of our recovered grandchildren. He helped to discover his legitimate parents.

(I recorded this testimony some months before Chicha Mariani presented her resignation as President of the Grandmothers.)

WHY WE WANT TO STRENGTHEN OUR IMPERFECT JUSTICE

Once again we go out into the streets:

The March to say NO to the amnesty.

Every time I rest my head on the pillow, all the images of those years appear. Everything speeds up. The children's blood that remains on the road neither dries up nor disappears: it accumulates. My weariness takes over but I am still able to think: we have to keep on fighting so that the need for justice is not just mine, but is on all our countrymen's consciences.

I find myself again among a multitude. I feel myself walking, and from my reduced space I realize that we are not alone. I cannot really quantify all this human tide. It fills me with admiration, because in spite of the profound economic crisis which weighs us down, people have spilled out into the street to scream their indignation along with us.

Again we come out into the streets. This time to say "NO TO THE AMNESTY."

On these days, when it looks as if a margin of justice has started to appear, the fight for the full force of human rights gains strength to oppose this new measure that the constitutional government proposes to adopt. President Menem, identified with the military and the other sectors of power, seems to want to satisfy once and for all the military demands by granting a general amnesty (parallel with the plan of "the Process").

For us the amnesty is a new piece of effrontery, a hard blow, because it means the pardoning of the military who were tried for extraordinary crimes, and it means, besides, that it will be impossible to continue with the cases already begun.

We found out that despite the president's enormous popularity, according to polls and inquiries there is a great majority against the pardoning of our oppressors. So we made the decision to carry out a march. All the human rights organizations and most of the political parties came together to organize the march against the amnesty.

On September 8 we left with other Mothers from the established spot in columns behind our sign. Because I was unwilling to leave my small space and my companions, I could not see the magnitude of the march. But I felt it consisted of a multitude such as had not joined us for a long time. What most impressed me was that at each street corner a human tide would come towards us to join the march. And to our astonishment, these were people who were self-motivated. Whole families came and accompanied us, as did people who were leaving work and on their way home.

Afterwards, through friends who had a fuller view of the march (because they had walked the length and the width of it while I was holding on to Graciela's picture poster without leaving my place) I started to perceive the magnitude of this convocation. The foreign news agencies estimated that two hundred thousand people participated in Buenos Aires alone. There were also marches in many of the cities in the provinces, including some where it was hard to think they would ever have them, like in Ushuaia and in Bariloche. Nevertheless, at the same time the citizens were mobilizing, the president reiterated his decision to grant the amnesty.

A few days later, on September 21, there was another moving event: a multitude celebrating the Day of the Student gathered around the pyramid after a call organized by the young people to reiterate the NO to the amnesty.

HASN'T ANYTHING CHANGED HERE?

Using four decrees dated October 6, the president granted amnesty to military men accused of homicide and torture, including their part in the Malvinas war, and to those involved in the Easter Week rebellion and those at Monte Caseros and Villa Martelli. They also included names of political militants, among them people who had been seen in clandestine concentration camps and who are among the disappeared and others who are known to be dead. In the midst of such irregularities, the President says that he assumes the political liabilities of the amnesty. It is a sorry outcome that brings to mind other cases of surrender by democratic governments over the issue of state terrorism.

The excuse for the reconciliation accepts the false idea that going around the Plaza protesting for our children means we are at war against our people. What it hides in its pretended holy facade is the transgression against the most solid principle on which our democratic system rests: justice.

This objective—domestic tranquility—as we supposed, is not being accomplished. Ordinary prisoners claim benefits similar to those granted to the political criminals. On the other hand, the military men who revolted do not accept being forced out, while the dignity of the political militants is violated by their being part of the same deal. Juan Gelman, the poet, asks himself: "How can I receive pardon side by side with my son's abductors and torturers?"

The struggle continues on both the legal and political terrain and reveals the impossibility of trying to hide by decree the most tragic period in our history.

THE PRESIDENT ANNOUNCES THE AMNESTY

The president of the nation, Carlos Saúl Menem, who in fact governs in monarchic style, has decided to privatize, sell, or give away the national inheritance accumulated by several generations. He is carrying out this plan hand-in-hand with the oligarchy, and this is producing the impoverishment of the people. Obviously, their desire to free all the military men who committed extraordinary crimes during the so-called "Process of National Reorganization" is only to be expected. These genocidal members of the armed forces have always retained the notion that they won the military but not the political war. This last amnesty grants them this very status, which they so much demanded. The new amnesty is also required for the repression needed to implement an economic plan of misery.

Note: As this book was coming out, President Menem announced the imminent pardon of the Junta members Videla, Massera, and Agosti, and of the former Montonero guerrilla leader, Firmenich. [MM]

TESTIMONIES

This is why I go to the circle,
the Plaza de Mayo circle —
for Raquel, for Pablo, for
Adriana, for....
who used to play in the schoolyard,
on the sidewalk.
The lamplighter,
the lamplighter stumbled...
To the circle, circle,
to the circle, circle, circle...
Forever.

A Tribute to Gustavo

I want to talk about our Gustavo. I want to tell you that we organized a tribute to him at my house. And I never thought that I would ever be able to fulfill my need, my yearning to talk about Gustavo, as if in all of our daily struggles something were still missing in our permanent search to find out what had happened to him. Goyo (his father) and I had decided that at some point we had to do it, but it was terribly difficult to dig even deeper into a wound that doesn't ever heal. We could not find the right place to do it. Finally, after much thinking and rethinking, we decided that our house should be the place.

Here in the house he shared with us, Gustavo lived his childhood, his adolescence, and as much as he lived of his youth. Here he was happy and made us happy with his gaiety, with the healthy drives of a boy, always aspiring to the best for himself and for everybody else. Sometimes I think that perhaps just because of that his life was so brief. The entire house is full of him, his things—the objects and the furniture, his records and his books, his poems, where he poured out all his feelings. He wanted to live in a just society, where men were free and he could express his thoughts. He knew there was much to be done, and he wanted to do it; he always worried about social injustices. His marvelous sensibility drove him to look at life with the desire to fight for the causes he considered fair. Sometimes I remember his chats with his friends, how they wanted to fix the world, to correct mistakes. What enthusiasm, what passion in their talk! How long they went on discussing

216

things! How much faith in life they had! We both, he and I, shared an enthusiasm for music; sometimes we sang or spent long periods listening to records. That's why when I listen to some of his favorites—I feel him next to me. This is the reason why I always feel the need to talk about Gustavo, even knowing how difficult it is and filled with the fear of choking and then not being able to talk. Everything turns out as if I were living again through childbirth: labor always preceded by tremendous pain, a pain as deep as it is vital, which is then transformed into a feeling of tranquility and peace; this is the peacefulness that my spirit so much seeks, and which only finds its gratification in remembering Gustavo's life. Gustavo left us a beautiful life-lesson.

He completed grammar school without any problem, and he got good marks at Urquiza High School, favoring the humanities. At that time he was an avid reader and knew how to select from the materials which fell into his hands. His vocation was the study of history in which he took great interest. We have a monograph he worked on along with another disappeared fellow-student—on Mexico and the agrarian reform. I remember that he looked at the work of many writers, which helps to explain his entering the School of Education to teach history in high school; we keep a paper he did there on the human races when he was 18 years old.

My statement is not just a matter of justifying all the kids who, like Gustavo, belonged to that generation; it is also a question of the responsibility of the parents. In our home conversations and comments on political subjects were habitual. As a child, Gustavo lived through the Martins and Zenteno Affair and, when he was a little bit older, the periods of the Triple A, Ortega Peña, Silvio Frondizi, Rucci, the happenings in Trelew, Ezeiza, Chile, Allende's death, and the problems at the universities. His participation at the Instituto del Profesorado de Historia's student center, to which he was a delegate, the living experiences of political prisoners and so much more formed Gustavo and his generation; they developed in this historical context; and to all of this can be added, within the frame of international politics, the consequences of the Vietnam war, the outbreaks in the Middle East, Peru's experience, etc. It is not fair to talk about these kids without being conscious of what I've just mentioned.

They said they were from the police

Gustavo felt the call of politics from a very early age, and it was very deep and encouraged by my husband who, from his youth, had been a politically active socialist. The library in our house was always available to Gustavo and there never was any kind of censorship; for that reason, he never hid anything, and we take responsibility for his moral and intellectual formation.

I think that my son of his own free will, like thousands of other kids, stood up before a generational obligation; he was not a stranger to the facts, his rebellion was fed by the injustices that he was living through; he didn't allow himself to be carried away, he criticized, he theorized, he questioned, and we have to respect his rebelliousness. After what we have lived through, I think Gustavo's crimes were those of being young, of thinking and of dissenting. This is why his generation suffered political indictment: the saying that "they were up to something"; such a cynical and perverse expression was aimed at wounding the parents, brothers, the whole family. They looked for a way to criminally mark a generation and to teach a lesson to all of us.

He wrote to express himself, he loved poetry and music. We have poems written by him on notebook pages. Once he gave me a book on my birthday, Gorky's *The Mother*, and his dedication is a poem.

There

Further away from time
and the words.
Further away from the routine
or Calvary.
Further away from the earthly,
the palpable, the concrete.
Further away, finally, from what's here,
Further away from the gray world.
Outside all this defined structure,
There is Love, there is Faith, there is Life...
...and there, there are mothers, our Mothers...
There, in our Hearts.
Much Happiness, Mom.

S. Pasik
Bs.As.8/7/74

I always have Gustavo's life with me, so full and so
beautiful. If we have survived, it is precisely because in self-
defense we have always relived that life to which Gustavo
gave himself as fully and completely as if he had no time to
waste. That is why, with a life so rich in feelings and goals, I
don't have to bring up how young he was. We have his life
so entrenched with us, that he will survive us; it is as if I
were telling you that our great pain is followed by the
greatness of my son's noble humanity.

Poor son, he was abducted on May 22, 1976 at dawn.
They took him from our own house at 6000 Juan B. Justo.
Five people in civilian clothes, carrying weapons and
claiming they belonged to the Federal Police, came to look
for him. They took Gustavo from our house, along with his
identity documents. They came in two Ford Falcons without licence plates. I remember that the credentials they

219

showed us proved to be false. And we were never officially told what became of him.

At first the pain daunted us. That lasted a long time. But as time went by, a very different spiritual need was born: I could not accept not being able to talk about Gustavo. I wanted him to be present with us, since his personality was so strongly felt within the family. That's why the need to review Gustavo's life became so strong for both his father and myself.

We achieved that purpose with a very intimate meeting of family and very close friends. It was the tribute dedicated to celebrating Gustavo's life I was telling you about at the beginning—at our house on a Sunday afternoon. Everybody participated. We read letters, poetry he wrote and left in his drawers, and he was with everybody in a memory or an anecdote. The meeting turned out to be as rich as it was overflowing with emotion. So it was that what at the beginning we thought could never be done, we were able to do quite naturally. It was for us an unforgettably satisfying experience.

I believe that the moment has arrived for me to put my own remembrances in order and to tell you of my own feelings. I too want to give my testimony about how they stole my daughter and how they turned me into one of the Mothers of the Plaza.

The smell of tragedy
had already begun to float in our surroundings

Gra looks tired out. She is sitting at the round table in the kitchen opposite her brother; they are holding back the tears in their eyes. She has fastened her gaze on the design on the plastic tablecloth. She presses one hand against the other until her nails dig in. Two big tears wet, then blur the flower on the table cloth. Without lifting her head, she says to me,

"You already know what's happened at Ezeiza. Please, out of respect for those kids who fell there, don't make any comments, criticisms or any sympathetic sighs. Just let's remain like this for a while."

I moved towards her and hugged her tightly.

"But mom! If we all leave,
who's going to remain?"

A few months before Graciela was taken, we had a birthday party for her grandmother. Graciela had just experienced a bit of a romantic disappointment. The party turned tense, I

221

saw she was terribly sad, very distressed; then, since she was staying at her grandmother's to sleep, I also wanted to remain. Graciela cried. From my bed, I could hear her crying. It took me some time to fall asleep and finally I had a dream. I dreamt that Graciela was being abducted; a number of men surrounded her, but the car they were putting her in was not the classic Ford Falcon, but a Fiat. And I was desperate, I ran after her...but then the dream vanished and a feeling of tragedy set in inside me, as if I were surrounded by a special atmosphere from which I could not escape. This happened in 1976, before the military coup.

I knew that Graciela had become militant. I didn't know what she was up to with any precision. I didn't ask questions, but I was sure that she visited "villas miserias." I saw it in her clothes and her muddy shoes when she returned and because she had told me that for her it was tremendously moving to get to know the villagers, who told her incredible stories about things which were totally different from her own life.

Since she had been very little Gra had always lived in comfortable places in the city. She was usually very well-dressed because her grandmother was a seamstress. I mean, the needs which she had, which were always satisfied, she observed in those people. What's more, because I believe she had a talent for writing, she used to recount to me the stories they told her.

One of the things she was getting from the villagers was that they were cheerful anyway and enjoyed the small pleasures they had within their reach. She used to say that when they were happy they were enviable—they could become happy with so little.

Gra was usually very busy, busy to the point of hysteria; I don't know if she liked or disliked what she was doing, but she never stopped going, and therefore was always very busy. She taught at private schools and was permanently on the go. She would return home completely exhausted. One of the beautiful things Graciela did for me was to tell me the stories about what was going on at the office. She would do this so well that I loved to listen to her, and I believe I could have easily recognized each one of her fellow workers if I came across them by chance. But I also felt sorry for her because I thought: Graciela is always talking about other people's lives, but she doesn't talk about her own.

We had many differences, we would quarrel a lot because both of us had very strong personalities, and sometimes we'd quarrel about nonsense. And I remember that once when we were talking about tangos, which she barely knew how to hum, I made her this proposition: "Well, when you graduate, you can learn to sing tangos, since you like them so much!" Gra said that once Perón returned, she would certainly learn to sing tangos. And I remember I once asked her, "What happened? You didn't learn to sing tangos." And she answered, "Actually, it's because the true Perón never came back."

During this stage there were two important moments in Graciela's life. The first was when she decided to become politically active, and the second when she decided to continue risking her life.

I don't believe that at the outset Graciela had a very clear idea of the danger they were risking when they took up the people's cause.

I believe that the period of terror had already started in 1975. Between the events unfolding and Graciela's comments, it became quite clear that she would get word of a detention, abduction, or a disappearance every time she ran into somebody on the street or at the university.

I believe that it was at this time that I started to become conscious that Graciela was in danger. I told her very clearly once: "This is beginning to produce a lot of anxiety, an awful lot, lots of mothers are going to live in a state of panic, and I also notice that lots of people are leaving the country." In any event, at that time we couldn't detect any encouraging signs, or anything that might give notice of change on the political scene. One day I made a very serious proposal to Graciela. "Why don't you leave, at least for a while?" And her answer was: "But Mom, if we all leave, who's going to stay? Well—it's a question of waiting until things become a bit clearer." So I suspect that at that moment she had an idea that she was running a risk, but thought that she shouldn't abandon her country....

At that time Graciela was living with a fellow student. I was absorbed by the many responsibilities of family life, and we didn't see each other so often. Besides, Graciela knew what was going on at home and didn't want to add to my worries.

Something else that alarmed me were *La Razon*'s headlines—in thick black letters: "Armed confrontation, Ten Persons Killed" or "Incident in Lanus: Four Subversives Shot." I also remember that they used to refer to incidents with drug addicts. But by this time our society was already turning into a totally hostile world plunged into terror.

It was a very, very long embrace

During the year-end holidays, we always met at home for a while. The children would go out with their friends to have a good time afterwards. The previous year (1975), we went out to the balcony to hear the sirens and Graciela and I embraced, embraced each other, but in such an incredible fashion that I still feel upon my neck the warmth of Graciela's dear face. It was a very, very long embrace. Graciela cried a lot. I contained my crying, but couldn't manage to contain my anguish. I believe that the two of us had a foreboding of the meaning of that embrace: we had a foreboding that it was an embrace which said goodbye.

And we didn't have another year-end together. Graciela was abducted on September 25, 1976.

Nine months went by between that embrace and the abduction. During that period, I saw her less, but I never stopped seeing her entirely; I felt an anxious need to be with her. Whenever she came into the house, I became very happy. I recognized it when she rang the bell. We would both chatter hurriedly, as if we didn't have enough time. There was always too little time to talk, but I tried to keep her abreast of what was going on at home.

I have very fresh in my mind the last time I saw her...it is as if it had just happened a few hours ago.... But before that last encounter, on September 14 we celebrated Graciela's birthday in a very amusing and pleasant way: Graciela, her brother, her sister-in-law, and me. Her father gave her a chain which she immediately put on. Graciela was very happy that evening.

I'll go back to that Saturday morning, September 24. Graciela calls me on the phone to arrange to meet at noon. We both take a seat in the sun at that plaza on Charcas and Cerrito Streets which has some ravines. It was a little bit cold. Graciela spoke rapidly and seemed to want to tell me a lot of things; I noticed that she had a sort of acne on her face for the very first time. Perhaps she had eaten something bad. Then the two of us laughed and voiced the same words: "You have to take...," I said "yeast," which was my constant maternal advice, and she said "bleach," and we both laughed a lot. She asked me about her grandmother and the rest of the family because by then we weren't seeing each other often at home. I had made some good things and I asked her to take them and share them with her friends. We parted after kissing and...well, I didn't have the feeling of a definitive separation, but afterwards I can assure you that I was unable to eat. The afternoon turned heavy, with the temperature climbing. Santiago and I lay down for the siesta. Around four in the afternoon, the

phone rang and someone asked if Graciela was there. I
asked again and again: "Who is it? Who is it?" "No," he
answered. "It's a friend," and that helped me afterwards to
make my own conjectures.

And all of a sudden, we were two poor devils...

Around six in the afternoon, Santiago decided to go to an
exhibit, but I didn't want to go because I tire easily and
preferred to attend an organ recital in San Telmo in the hall
of a very old house. The organist was to interpret the piece
followed by a discussion by a musicologist. Immediately
upon lining up to get the ticket, I started to feel ill, I didn't
know why I felt so poorly—a feeling of being very tired, as
if I had a great weight on me, and then I went in. And
around six or half-past six, I felt as if I were sinking, sinking deep in the earth, I felt breathless and had a sensation
of darkness, horror, and anguish. And I was unable to
shake off any of this, but I tried to bear it until the end of
the recital. I went back, not home, but to Graciela's
grandmother's house. I found my husband there, and we
started walking slowly towards our place but decided to go
into one of the movie houses on Callao Street. We were just
about to get the tickets when I said I didn't feel like it, that I
had a great urge to go back home. I could not eat that
evening either. We retired to bed and suddenly a horrible,
violent ringing of the doorbell wrenched both of us from
our sleep, and then another assault began: the search and
seizure of my home. The first thing I remember is their
screaming at me: "We've come for your daughter," using a
very harsh, merciless tone of voice. At that moment, I
honestly thought: "If you're looking for her, ah! I hope you
haven't found her." Afterwards, the minutes that followed
made up a night of horror; everything they said was false, a
lie. They told me: "We've come to find your daughter, she is

226

a subversive." But I suspect now that Graciela had already been abducted some time after three or three-thirty in the afternoon. I do not understand the events of Graciela's abduction clearly. I do know that she was abducted on the street in the Almagro neighborhood, I believe together with other people, and I know positively that it was at that time, but that's all.

From my house they took me to an empty apartment of ours which we were about to sell; there they did another very violent search and seizure. They used some grenades to blow out the door. They had me with them; they asked me to ring the apartment's bell because they thought that there were people inside. What I remember is that I approached the door and rang the bell. At that moment I thought: "They would shoot the two of us, myself on this side, and Graciela—if she were there on the other side of the door." All of these people were heavily armed. After that they took me to the house of one of my sisters, they invaded the house of those poor people, who were sleeping, my brother-in-law was sick.... It was an operation which lasted around an hour. Afterwards, back again to my house. When they left me at home...it's so incredible now, so absurd...one of these totally unknown strangers asked me: "And now what are you going to do?" At that moment I felt like an automaton. I looked at him like an idiot and I told him something like: "I suppose I'm going to lie down and cry, I don't know." And they left. But I didn't sit down and cry. We went over the house. It was devastated, papers, notebooks, books thrown on the floor—all over the place. They had also taken away a large number of notebooks and university folders, some from high school, and even from grade school, appointment books with addresses, photos. My husband and I were left alone. It was dawn.... We threw ourselves on the bed. He fell into a stupor for a while. I sat on the bed and each noise I heard from the street made me jump; there was no longer any peace for me. On the following night, we tried to sleep, but we couldn't, and after the next night, we decided to leave, because this place got us into such a state of anxiety, we felt almost suffocated. We would look at all the things, the objects thrown on the floor...it seems we were afraid of more violence, and we couldn't rest, we couldn't eat. We had to gather all our courage to get dressed and go out to let our family know and to ask for help. It was Sunday, the day after the abduction. We went out into the street like two zombies and started to walk. At times we grabbed each other's hand very tightly, then we'd let go, at times we'd walk arm in arm... and we kept on walking. We would see a public phone, and want to make a call, but we couldn't remember the numbers; suddenly I remembered my daughter-in-law's mother's number, and I told them what had happened. I asked for the children not to come because I was afraid. They were very fearful too because they didn't come to see us.

And all of a sudden, from one day to the next, we were two poor souls walking, abandoned, perplexed, through an absolutely deserted city (it was siesta time). I felt like lying down in the middle of the street. We found it hard to walk, tasting our bitterness. We knew that any word that either one of us might say could demolish the other. We didn't realize that this night of terror was for us the beginning of a merciless torture: the wait without any news. And that it was going to last long years.

What a strange feeling we had. In this same city where both of us, the mother and father of Graciela, had been born, we were like foreigners. Everything was different and unrecognizable: streets, plazas, parks. Everything was solitary and mute, and both of us sank into an intense, anguished forlornness.

And now, what do we do?

As the hours passed, we started to reflect and to think
about lawyers. We turned to a neighbor, an old politician of
Avellaneda's time. We asked him if he had heard the
previous night's uproar. He said very calmly that he hadn't.
I didn't believe it for a minute. It was impossible not to
have heard. But he told me he had no doubt it had been an
abduction like the ones that were so abundant those days.
Then I wept and wept and asked him what the possibilities
were of finding out what had happened to Graciela. He
promised to look into it, and that was my first hope, and I
held on to it in despair. Then I remembered that when they
came into the house they screamed: "If we don't find her
here, you won't find her either, or if you do, you'll find her
in the morgue." That's what they told me: "You'll find her
in the morgue." But after so much searching, I didn't find
her in the morgue either. I want to say that in spite of all
the time that's gone by, my daughter continues to be
disappeared, and though everything makes one suppose
that she was killed, I am waiting to find her, even in the
morgue. I am waiting to hear the exact truth about what
happened to her. They owe me this, as they owe it to all the
Mothers.

During those first days, we lived through many trials. I
don't know how we found out that there was an office at
the Casa Rosada which was under the Ministry of the
Interior where everybody went to ask if they knew anything
about their son or daughter who had been carried away
and hadn't been seen again. And that was where Santiago
went to ask and where he met a man wearing a black tie
who said: "Ah! The subversives caused me a lot of grief. Do
you see this black tie? It's because they killed my father."
Santiago told him that he was sorry, but that at that moment he wanted to ask for news about his daughter, and
the man said: "But you are telling me that they asked you

for your daughter's photograph. It's very clear," the man
continued sarcastically: "She must have escaped and that's
why they asked you for Graciela's photo." When my
husband came home, he was so dazed that he told me:
"Look, let's grant ourselves the possibility that they're still
looking for her." And that so enraged me that I felt like
attacking him, like striking him. "But how can you think,
how can you imagine that Graciela wouldn't do something
to let us know—to communicate with us? She's been
kidnapped, there's no doubt about it." But we didn't know
what steps to take, we simply didn't know what to do. So
we started looking for a lawyer. We went to our family
lawyer, who told us that in these cases a writ of habeas
corpus was what was needed, but he was hesitant about
getting involved, he didn't want to compromise himself. He
told us everything he knew and had heard about other
cases, and of what had happened to the uncle, the cousin,
or to Tom, Dick and Harry. We had to use those stories as a
basis on which to move. Finally he agreed to write the
habeas corpus, but his cowardice was such that he told us:
"You can present it yourselves, but I will go to the court
house with you." He accompanied Graciela's father up to
four blocks away from the court house. Then he told him
where he had to go to present this document—we had
never before heard a word about it—this "habeas corpus."
Santiago later told of a fellow at the court house typing
away with a cold air about him, because, he explained, on
that day there had already been ten or fifteen—I don't
remember exactly how many—habeas corpuses. Then
Santiago asked him if there was a possibility the judge
could find out anything, and the fellow answered: "Look, to
be frank, I don't think so...." And Santiago told me that
right then and there he started crying like a child, he cried
right over the typewriter, right over the desk with his
habeas corpus ready in his hands.

That's what the days were like following Graciela's disappearance.

With all the details that we had and all we were reading in the newspapers, we knew what was really going on in the country, so that we had to stuff the terror and the horror in our pockets, try to calm ourselves, and go out and search for Graciela. We looked for her every way we could, but there weren't many possibilities—from that of contacting a lawyer to that of establishing contact with one politician or another, to looking for a friend of Graciela's to find out if he knew anything. But then I remembered an old friend of Graciela's and I asked him to meet me at a bar. It was Antonio Brailovsky. I had doubts he'd want to meet me, but he did. He must have found me demented and desolated because the first thing he said was something like: "Matilde, you have to fix yourself up a little bit, to comb your hair." And the second thing he recommended was for me to look for one of those women who reads cards or for a fortune teller. That seemed pretty crazy to me, but these were his exact words: "When you are in a state of terror, you don't know anything, absolutely nothing about anything. In the midst of absolute darkness, the best thing is to get some word." Cursing, I left him, but I'd heard what he had told me.

I came to the conclusion they had killed them all

Five days after Graciela's abduction, I received a telephone call. My sister-in-law answered it, but she gestured to me and I immediately picked up the phone. A man's voice said: "Am I speaking to telephone number such and such? Just a moment, they're going to talk to you...." Then I heard Graciela's voice, no doubt about it. It was a voice...I would say...an almost happy voice: "Aunt! Aunt!"—she said—

"This is Graciela!" Since I was all but living at her grandmother's, she must have called home and got no answer. "No, dear"—I answered—"it's not your aunt, it's Mom! Where are you? Where are you, my love?" Then her voice began to change: "I'm very far away, I think I'm very far away." I understood it was going to be a very brief call and I asked her: "When am I going to see you? Am I going to see you again?" And she told me: "No, no Mom, never again...."

I don't recall her exact words after that, but she told me in a voice filled with emotion: "Mom, I love you, I love you...." And I had the strength to answer: "And I adore you and I am with you, wherever you are, I am with you...." And they cut off the communication, but before they cut it off I realized that Graciela's voice was becoming very weak. So I thought I don't know what—that they were torturing her or...I don't know, I don't know....

I also thought that she was under the effects of some injection, since at the beginning her voice sounded very strong, but then no longer so. After this call, I started to run into the streets like a madwoman....

Around that time I had already met a priest who was receiving family members day and night, and my sister-in-law had run after me. We went to tell him what had just happened. It took a long time until he saw me. The call must have been at about four in the afternoon and when I managed to talk to him it must have been about eight. He looked at me in disbelief, as if I were lying to him, and he said to me: "But why would they want to do such a thing? Because that would be really sadistic, right? I don't believe it, but...." The only concrete thing he told me was: "Well, up to today, Graciela is alive."

Overcoming my emotion, at times I thought that it had been a dream. Ah! I had so many dreams afterwards, so many nightmares, and I spoke with Graciela so many times in my dreams.... But there is no chance that it had been a dream, because there were so many people right by me who heard me talking on the phone, who can attest to this report.

Later I heard that other people had received similar calls. I started to investigate why it had been done, what the objective was, and I was given several explanations, some of them wild, others containing some logic, until after a long time, maybe three or four months later, I spoke to a well-known old priest, Iñaki de Aspiazu, who said to me: "Yes, yes, that call means that they have Graciela, and they did it because we told them that they had to write a note saying where the detained were, so that at least their families would know; we told them this many times. We thought that they could tell the families by means of a note, but they said that there was no time for notes."

Graselli, a priest everybody used to go to, offered me another version. He told me that the call's objective was to apply psychological pressure. The effects of that phone call didn't go away, it has never left me.... And so, after her disappearance, Graciela symbolically calls me and I hear her at the other end of the line, but it's a call still without an answer. It is one more thing I have pending, that call is still unfinished.

I was able to see very few of Graciela's friends. I didn't see Antonio very often; I found him a fellow who tried to hide his emotions, but who at the same time wanted to keep me company. I found him to be full of good sense, and he offered so much affection with his eyes, that when I got back home after seeing him, I would think: "Well, here's somebody who can think more calmly and who can give me ideas about how to survive, so let's pay more attention to him." Each time I saw Antonio, afterwards I felt my legs becoming firmer and stronger so that I could continue the search. Besides, I thought that he was saner than me, and because of his activities, he had a clearer picture of the situation than me. Among all Graciela's friends, very few came near us. A bitter moment arrived when I told myself: "They must have killed them all...they kill so many people...."

We started to spread the news of Graciela's disappearance through the newspapers, Amnesty International, and every other place we could think of. What we wanted immediately was for the whole world to know about Graciela's disappearance. We spread the word to all the institutions in our community, to everybody....

There was a plaza near Graciela's school...

One of the things that terrified me when I'd go out walking in the evenings—so as not to stay home crying—were the newspapers in the kiosks, which announced all the armed confrontations and the many deaths in bold print.

Actually, I already had no doubts about the nonexistence of such confrontations; I was sure they were referring to cases like ours. And I started to buy all the newspapers and magazines being published. I'd put everything aside and I would read them avidly. But the only thing I'd find were references to these supposed confrontations, not anything about what had really taken place. Of course not. I bought the *Buenos Aires Herald* once. I wasn't familiar with it because it was an English language newspaper; however in an editorial written in Spanish I discovered mention of some people who met at the Plaza de Mayo. It didn't explain their purpose, but this was during a time when we were under a state of siege. I felt it had something to do with me. To start with, I had no idea how to approach them. Then I thought of taking one of the buses which circled the Plaza de Mayo on its route. I started to take it at different times and on different days...and I'd look out the windows. I would look out, filled with great anxiety, but failed to see anything abnormal, until one day a small group of people, huddled very close together as if in discussion, caught my attention. One could see that they were into something other than an outing. I got off at the first stop, but unluckily, when I got near, the group had already separated. I imagined that they were the people I had read about in the *Herald*. Anyway, I had discovered their day and their time.

The following week I returned to the Plaza, and, to be sure, they were there. I got near them, but I didn't dare ask anything. I returned once or twice. I noticed that they were looking at me, but in the same way that I was looking at the pigeons. Nobody was paying any real attention to me. I didn't know anybody and I thought they were looking at me suspiciously, or that they assumed that I was simply a curious busybody.

By this time, I had already met the Westerkamps. These people had a son in Sierra Chica prison. He had disappeared a short time earlier, but had been "white washed," and he subsequently reappeared in that jail. Angela Westerkamp became one of my best friends, a relationship that we have kept up. I decided to go to see her and to explain that I very much wanted to go to the Plaza. She put me in contact with Chela Mignone. I went to her house a half an hour before the Plaza meeting. Chela gave me a very warm reception since I came recommended, but on the other hand, this didn't stop her from asking me questions. She also was living in this climate of suspicion in which all of us were living. We took a subway train, line A, and she kept on asking me questions. I answered, telling her in detail about the search and seizure, who we were.... So we got out of the subway station together. At that moment she said to me: "Well, now we separate, I will be walking behind you keeping my eyes open." Subsequently we did the same thing two or three times. I believe that at that time they were already doing the circle, and I joined because of the fact that I was with Chela, who was one of the fourteen first

Mothers. But to say joining a group is not precisely accurate either, because it is very difficult for me to become part of a group, and to join that one was even more difficult. Nevertheless, I contemplated them with great hope, with great affection. I remember that they filled me with a profound admiration, and I told myself: "They are already doing something. I cannot come out of my state of suspended animation, of my paralysis, but they have determined to get back their children." I had discovered them by reading the *Buenos Aires Herald*. By then its director, Robert Cox, had turned into a defender of human rights, despite the fact that his newspaper was quite a conservative one.

Another thing that impressed me at the Plaza was seeing some of those faces. Some of the women were very weepy and very desperate, and others were clearly hysterical. It scared me a bit...they shouted and cursed. It was odd that from that spot, just across from the real seat of government, they felt that they could do this.

It astonished me to see that many of the Mothers knew perfectly well the names of some of the military or the people who took their children; one shouldn't forget that when the military burst into our houses dressed in civilian clothes, they used aliases to address each other.

Nevertheless, these Mothers mentioned many of their names, and they repeated them incessantly. This was what the atmosphere at the Plaza was like, permeated as well by a feeling of rage and above all, great pain—a shared pain.

And it was in this way that my routine of going around the pyramid in Plaza de Mayo started; and it is not yet over. Afterwards, I awaited the arrival of the following Thursday filled with incredible anxiety; and when the day arrived, I thought about the walk around the pyramid. When I'd wake up...not when I'd wake up because I did not sleep through the whole night...but when I jumped out of bed, I would make all sorts of preparations so as to arrive on time, because the time spent there was very brief and I was afraid of arriving early and being alone. I would hide it all from my husband. I hid it for some time and, of course, from the children's grandmother because by then the family was reduced to only that: their grandmother, an aunt, their father, and me. At that time, going to the Plaza was a cause of great anxiety for me because there was always the possibility that some Mother had received some news, and the Mothers were the only people I trusted....

Then afterwards, there was the problem of leaving the Plaza. It was another source of anxiety: we were afraid, we were careful, we would disperse very quickly, one by one; we would never leave in groups of two or three—never. We tried to reach Avenida de Mayo or Florida Street quickly, because that made us feel more secure. The men of the "process" cared about their image, so they avoided carrying out violent detentions on the street, but I believe that they followed us and kept us under surveillance. We all shared the same notion about this, especially at the Plaza. We were aware of it, and we also recognized that we were across from the Casa Rosada, which is the country's political center. They would take pictures of us, but that didn't scare us enough to decide to stop coming back. Just the opposite. It seemed that it was the only place where we could plan things, and it was there that we gestated ideas.

What I know with certainty is that by denying us any information to allow us to find our children, they made us come up with new strategies. And one of our new strategies was not to stop the walk.

When I say that they closed every door to us, this is not just a metaphor, not at all. Many times when we were in the Plaza and had suffered from one aggressive act or another and needed to take refuge somewhere, we headed for the Cathedral across the street but, in general, we found it closed. I clearly remember Dora, "Tana," one of our old companions, knocking with both fists on the Cathedral doors and shouting: "Skirt-wearers, let us in!"—and I know she is a fervent Catholic, a strong believer.

And just at that moment, people from other human rights organizations who participated in the circle were approaching, as well as mothers, family members, people from the Assembly, from MEHD, CELS....

Remembering Gra

To talk about Graciela at this moment moves me. Graciela had a very strong character, very vibrant, very vital. There were different stages in our relationship. A very long stage, starting during her adolescence, was one of misunderstandings. We criticized each other a lot, Graciela demanded a lot from me. But luckily for me, we finally became very good friends, with a great tenderness in our friendship.

What is Graciela like? What is Graciela like physically, what was her character like? In my dreams, in my frequent dreams, I reexperience Graciela, but it is remarkable, it's not always the same face, nor is she the same age, nor is her frame of mind always the same. I reexperience Graciela's numerous faces, sometimes the very distinctive smile she had when she agreed to something, another time her smile of amusement, another her face of disgust. Graciela had many aspects, like everybody. She had many moods, and she passed rapidly from a happy to a sad mood. Some moments spent together were really so amusing that I will never forget them. We didn't have to invent games during our short moments together, because, anyway, we couldn't spend much time together.

But Graciela also had some moments of great impatience. We would start chatting in a very lively way, and all of a sudden Gra would look at her watch and become impatient, hysterical, and bam—the conversation was over, but just like that!—with a slam of the door, "Bye"...and we both would dash off.

I don't want to idealize Gra as if she were a perfect human being. I want to remember her with all her faults and weaknesses, because that's the way we loved her. She was totally obsessive about her work, really obsessive. When she was studying she was obsessive, not for the grade, but for the fulfillment of her task. And when she committed herself to something, it was exactly the same.

And there were other quite negative things about her, but in general, Gras was fun. I remember that she was very jealous, and that she suffered because of that. Maybe she was excessively jealous of the people she loved, of her friends. She deeply loved her grandmothers: I would go as far as to say they were her weakness. If I complained about my mother, she would become annoyed and say: "Careful, don't speak ill of my grandmother." And if I made a comment about my mother-in-law, she would say: "She's your mother-in-law, but don't forget, she's my grand-mother." She adored them. I think it's curious how many things they passed on to her. Well, she liked children a lot, babies, the children she never managed to have. She used to play with them, playing as if she were one of them, having a lot of fun, enjoying herself in their company.

Gra went to grammar school in Villa del Parque, the neighborhood where she was born. Then she did her secondary education at the National High School in Buenos Aires, one of the second group of women who graduated from it, because it had traditionally been a boy's school. The school made a very strong impact on Gra, it came to be part of her life, and it is there that she met her closest friends. I think that all this had a lot to do with the shaping of her character and ideals.

After she graduated from High School, she became a student at the University of Buenos Aires. There she graduated with a degree in Political Economy. She then worked as a translator at Amorrortu, was employed by the Editorial Center, and, finally, got a position at the office of State Water and Energy, a job from which she was removed. We didn't know at that time that to be fired from a job like that was very dangerous. Gra complained to the authorities and said that she would prefer to tender her resignation and for them to accept it. But, how ridiculous!—the official envelope containing the acceptance of her resignation didn't arrive at our house until after Gra's disappearance.

Gra was always full of well-planned projects. Hardly two years before her disappearance, I arrived home one day and approached the bathroom where Gra was putting on her makeup. She had already served me a *mate* because I was very tired, and I remained leaning against the bathroom doorway looking at her. She observed me through the mirror and told me very calmly that she was thinking of doing this or that having to do with her profession. She told this to me with much determination and enthusiasm. And I was looking at her while she fixed herself up, convinced that she was going to do all these things. It's just that neither of us suspected then that the period of repression would not give her time for anything.... But on that day I looked at her with admiration.... I don't know why she used makeup on those beautiful eyes, shaped like a dove's wing and exactly the same color of burnt sugar. She really didn't need it. I found her so attractive as she got ready to go out. She knew she was attractive. She had a nice figure, a long torso and a small waist. She was tall and had wavy dark brown hair.

When Gra came into the house, everything would light up. Each wall and each object took on meaning. The whole house would seem to sway as if it were a house of cards. Everything acquired energy, life, and noise. Noise above all: "I've lost a notebook! Mom, help me with the curler for my hair! Just leave the phone alone, it's for me! Turn on the oven, I've learnt to make the cheapest dessert! Look at the shirt I bought for my brother! Are you going by the post office?"

Because she was always in such a hurry, she drew two large ears with a black marker on the sides of the electric intercom to the building's entryway...why? "So that you can hear it faster!" From this I acquired the mania of writing on the walls...drawing...I drew her image, and now I write things, things that only I can understand. It is one of my ways of being with Gra.... And toward the end when she was going out, we would start quarreling. Ah, if I only could quarrel a little bit with her now, just a little bit!

"Where's my beige coat?" I asked her, making fun of her before she had a chance, because I knew her answer beforehand: "I needed it. Look mom, you have three coats, you won't be any colder outside because you're missing one...." I'd complain: "Then why didn't you take the oldest one?" "Well, the one I took was the nicest and it looks better on the person I gave it to. She needs to be presentable for the new job she got...."

I've never managed to do it—I've never managed to remember the horrible night of the abduction without evoking Graciela within myself, her personality—without ceasing to hear her voice. It doesn't matter how much time goes by, when I remember that day's events, I inevitably hear Graciela speaking. The two of us have told this story together. And what's more; even now we continue to disregard and interrupt each other....

EPILOGUE

"I imagine hell not as a place containing iron beds with nails where the condemned have to lie, but a place with some comfortable chairs where you sit waiting at ease for the postman...the person who brings news which will never come."

These words stirred me deeply because I saw that they described one of our worse punishments, punishments imposed upon us. I found them in a short story by Singer and it proved to me that somebody besides us knew of the horrendous anguish produced by the uncertain and interminable waiting for news.

During my loneliest moments, I imagine that Gra blew this book's contents into my ear, and also the reverse, that with it I am desperately trying to reach her with a message telling her how much I have searched for her and that I am still searching for her. I would like to ask her forgiveness, and that of all her companions, for our incompetence, and to let them know, wherever they are, that we can't forget them and that we will never forget them.

For this book is also a message to all the mothers in the country and in the world, and even to those who are just being born: I want them to know that when they tried to turn us into a marginalized group of imbeciles, we didn't retreat into seclusion; instead we went out to scream our pain and to protest in every corner of the world because we rejected being condemned to a chair. All the anguish and the suffering was turned into energy, and that energy into movement.

This will be an open-ended book. Surely our disappeared are already murmuring in the consciences of our people about new ways for demanding justice....

> *Each kerchief is a life that stirs in my memory.... I keep seeing them jumping between my flower beds with their obstinate faith, with their limitless gaiety, with their demands for change, so that justice will really be the rule.... I see them when I see their Mothers, who won't desert me.... I see Dalmiro Flores, that boy shot in cold blood at the end of the first March of Multitudes against the dictatorship, on December 16, 1982.... I feel that our children are telling their Mothers not to abandon him. Dalmiro, from his birth to his death, was condemned to be marginalized by a society stubbornly defending its privileges. Dalmiro didn't have a neighborhood, or friends, not even a mother with a white kerchief demanding that they pay the price for his death.*

Listen everybody. Listen to the voices I hear: the voices no longer crying in my circle, voices of hope which keep urging the dawn of a new world.

THE CIRCLE

To the circle, the circle.
to the circle, the circle, of small jumps,
of songs, of laughter,
the circle, my boy, my girl,
my girl...the circle...
What's her name?
She jumps and she laughs in the circle
in the playground,
and on the loose-tiled sidewalk,
she sings of the Lantern Lady...
The Lantern Lady stumbled...
Her name? Adriana?
Yes, her name might be Adriana,
Adriana with the ding-dong of little bells,
or Raquel? Why not?
My girl, my daughter, Adriana, Raquel,
or Pablo, my son, Pablo, my son,
in the circle, bright eyes,
The Lantern Lady...
The silent, slow, concentrated circle,
us, the women in dark clothes,
with dark looks,
us, the women who walk in circles,
myself a woman, myself a mother,
in Adriana's name,
in Pablo's,
in Raquel's,
for my son, for my daughter,
Me, a mother in the circle under the white caress
of a kerchief,
a white kerchief with an inscription:
a name, a date.
The small handkerchiefs...
with embroidered flowers, with boats,
with Mickey Mouse,

painted on with indelible paint,
the small handkerchiefs half-stuck
in a little pocket,
the dirty noses
and the circle of laughter,
the circle, the circle of childhood,
and me, a mother in this somber circle
at the Plaza de Mayo,
me, who cries no longer,
— though sometimes in hiding,
but in hiding —,
because in the circle at the Plaza de Mayo
I don't cry, I look at them with dry eyes,
I look at you who look at me,
who perhaps would like to know,
and I, from my tremendous clarity,
I, from my insomnia,
will ask you
if you have any children,
you, with the camera,
you, in the uniform,
do you have any children?
do you have children with the names of bells?
Me?
I don't know.
I don't know.
That's why I go back to the circle,
the Plaza de Mayo circle,
for Raquel, for Pablo, for Adriana, for...
who used to play in the playground,
on the sidewalk,
The Lantern Lady,
The Lantern Lady stumbled...
To the circle, the circle,
To the circle, the circle, the circle...
forever.

—Hebe Naes

Names and Terms

AAA or Triple A: Alianza Anticomunista Argentina [Argentine Anticommunist Alliance]. An organization most active during the Peronist Government after the elections of March 1973. It was formed by right-wing elements of the Peronist Party and elements of the Army and Federal Police. Its leader was José López Rega, strongman in the Perón Circle and advisor of Isabel Perón during her administration.

Raul Alfonsín: The democratically elected president who took over in 1983 from the third and last military Junta whose president was Lt. General Leopoldo Galtieri.

Ricardo Balbín (1904-1981): The long-time leader of the Radical Party. In only one election was he able to contest the presidency, which he lost to Perón in September 1973. He was imprisoned twice during Videla's term in office. He died in 1981.

CELS: Centro de Estudios Legales y Sociales (Center for Legal and Social Studies), an organization led by Emilio Mignone, who had been a minister during one of the '60s military governments. His daughter was killed after being arrested at her father's house.

CONADEP: Comisión Nacional Sobre la Desaparición de Personas (The National Commission on Missing Persons).

Patricia Derian: Coordinator for Human Rights and Humanitarian Affairs during President Carter's administration.

Easter Week Rebellion, March 16, 1987: The crisis originated with the resistance of junior Army officers in response to the Criminal Justice trials concerning their participation in human rights violations. President Alfonsín ended it by going to the barracks and negotiating. In return for the surrender of its leader, Lt. Col. Rico, Congress passed, in June 1987, Alfonsín's Law of Due Obedience. In January 1988, Rico escaped from detention and appeared in Monte Caseros (Corrientes Province) heading its mutinous regiment. After four days, surrounded by Army troops, he surrendered and was again imprisoned. December 1988, in Villa Martelli, there was a rebellion under Col. Ali Seinedin. It attempted to: 1) liberate Lt. Col. Rico, 2) end the trials, 3) gain amnesty for the condemned officers and, 4) gain better salaries. There was unrest in other regiments as well. Finally Col. Seinedin surrendered. The Army got a 40% salary increase and the Commander of the Army was changed. Afterwards, Lt. Col. Rico and Col. Seinedin begin their political careers.

Adolfo Pérez Esquivel: President of Paz y Justicia (Peace and Justice), a human rights organization openly opposed to the Malvinas war. He was imprisoned from 1976 to 1979. He received the Nobel Peace Prize in 1980.

Ezeiza, December 16, 1982: At Perón's return form Spain, a great number of people representing the left, center and right factions of the Peronist party gathered to receive him at Ezeiza Airport in Buenos Aires. A large number of the leftist group were gunned down without the security forces doing anything to stop the massacre.

Silvio Frondizi: Brother of former President Arturo Frondizi (1958-62), a leftist intellectual and academic killed by the AAA.

Albano Hargindeguy: General of the Army, Minister of the Interior in charge of the Federal Police during the first military junta.

General Leopoldo Galtieri: President of the third junta, succeeding Gen. Viola. He took the country to war against Britain over the Malvinas (Falkland Islands). The defeat forced the armed forces to call for elections, which were won by Alfonsín.

General Juan Lavalle (1797-1841): In 1828 he took over the government of the Province of Buenos Aires and had its elected governor, General Dorrego, executed without a trial in spite of advice to the contrary.

Castro Madero: Admiral of the Navy, President of the National Commission of Atomic Energy.

Martins and Zenteno Affair: Martins and Zenteno were two lawyers, partners in the defense of political prisoners during the Onganía-Lanusse military dictatorship (1966-1973). In 1972 they were kidnapped and killed.

Adm. Emilio E. Massera and Gen. Orlando Agosti, together with Gen. Videla, formed part of the first Junta which assumed power after the March 24, 1976 coup deposing Isabel Perón's government. They represented the three branches of the armed forces: Navy, Air Force and Army respectively.

MEHD: Movimiento Ecuménico por los Derechos Humanos (Ecumenical Movement for Human Rights), a Methodist led organization supported mainly by German religious organizations.

General Luciano Benjamín Menendez: Commandant of the 3rd. Army Corps in Córdoba, which controls all the Northeastern region of the country.

Mariano Moreno (1778-1811): Lawyer, politician, diplomat, secretary of Argentina's first Junta (1809). In 1810 he voted against keeping Viceroy Cisneros and thus for Argentina's separation from Spain. He founded the newspaper *La Gaceta* and contributed to the ideologic, political and economic orientation of the country. He was opposed to the unification of Latin America. He died at seas on his way to London to realize a diplomatic mission.

Ruiz Palacios: Subsecretary at the Ministry of the Interior.

Osvaldo Papaleo: A right-wing Peronist, newspaperman, TV anchorman.

Ortega Pena: A lawyer, national deputy and leftist. He was assassinated by the AAA while he was a member of Congress.

Jose Rucci: Secretary General of the Confederación General del Trabajo [General Confederation of Labor], which is Argentina's umbrella labor syndicate. Rucci was part of Perón's inner circle. Montoneros accused him of selling out the workers and killed Rucci on September 24, 1973, claiming they wished to free the newly reelected Perón and his Vice-President, Isabel Perón, from negative influences; the result was a deep split between Perón and Montoneros.

Trelew: Location of Rawson Prison in the province of Chubut, 1400 kilometers from Buenos Aires, where some hundred political prisoners were being held. In August, 1972, during the Lanusse Government, members of several important revolutionary organizations took over the prison to liberate their leaders. They also managed to take over a regular airline flight at the Trelew Airport. The rescued prisoners and the rescuers had trouble reaching the airport, and the plane had to depart. Sixteen were left stranded at the airport, surrounded, and taken prisoner by naval forces from a nearby base. The plane landed in Chile with Cuba as its final destination. Those who failed to make it were lined up and shot on August 22, 1972, and are known as "the martyrs of Trelew."

Jorge Rafael Videla: President of the first Junta, who took over the government with a coup on March 24, 1976.

Roberto Viola: President of the second junta, succeeded Gen. Videla.

TERMS:

hood: The abducted were taken from their places wrapped in a blanket with a hood over their heads. The hood was left on for the purpose of making it impossible for them to see their abductors, the places they were taken to, their torturers, and maintaining them in a state of disorientation.

mate: An infusion of dried mate leaves covered with hot water and drunk from a gourd through a "bombilla," a metal tube provided at the lower end with a strainer.

parsley: A prison term given to a prisoner who had a marginal role or simply an acquaintance with members of revolutionary organizations. After being kidnapped and useful information had been obtained, they were "legalized" (freed), sent to regular prisons or killed.

Punto final: A statute of limitations giving a sixty-day period to request investigation of those who may be responsible for crimes concerning human rights.

sucking center: Clandestine place where the abducted were kept hooded, shackled, and subjected to torture.

249

Curbstone Press, Inc.

is a non-profit publishing house dedicated to literature that reflects a commitment to social change, with an emphasis on contemporary writing from Latin America and Latino communities in the United States. Curbstone presents writers who give voice to the unheard in a language that goes beyond denunciation to celebrate, honor and teach. Curbstone builds bridges between its writers and the public – from inner-city to rural areas, colleges to community centers, children to adults. Curbstone seeks out the highest aesthetic expression of the dedication to human rights and intercultural understanding: poetry, testimonials, novels, stories, photography.

This mission requires more than just producing books. It requires ensuring that as many people as possible know about these books and read them. To achieve this, a large portion of Curbstone's schedule is dedicated to arranging tours and programs for its authors, working with public school and university teachers to enrich curricula, reaching out to underserved audiences by donating books and conducting readings and community programs, and promoting discussion in the media. It is only through these combined efforts that literature can truly make a difference.

Curbstone Press, like all non-profit presses, depends on the support of individuals, foundations, and government agencies to bring you, the reader, works of literary merit and social significance which might not find a place in profit-driven publishing channels. Our sincere thanks to the many individuals who support this endeavor and to the following organizations, foundations and government agencies: ADCO Foundation, Witter Bynner Foundation for Poetry, Connecticut Commission on the Arts, Connecticut Arts Endowment Fund, Ford Foundation, Greater Hartford Arts Council, Junior League of Hartford, Lawson Valentine Foundation, LEF Foundation, Lila Wallace-Reader's Digest Fund, The Andrew W. Mellon Foundation, National Endowment for the Arts, Samuel Rubin Foundation and the Puffin Foundation.

Please support Curbstone's efforts to present the diverse voices and views that make our culture richer. Tax-deductible donations can be made by check or credit card to Curbstone Press, 321 Jackson St., Willimantic, CT 06226 Tel: (860) 423-5110.